INSIDE
THE
CIRCLE

YOU!

How To Make Simple, Intentional Decisions
To Better Your Life And Income

By Andy Albright

Designed by Ryan Wagner

ISBN: 978-0-9973786-0-3

Printed in the United States of America

Visit my website at AndyAlbright.com. Thank You!

DEDICATION

This book is dedicated to my parents, who raised me with strong values, a solid work ethic and the belief that anything is possible when you put your mind to it.

To my late father, George Albright (below right), who instilled in me a work ethic and drive to get the job done no matter what it took.

To my mother, Laverne (below left), who has always believed and told people that if I set my mind to doing something then watch out, because "Andy can do anything." Thanks for always having confidence in me to be successful!

Table Of Contents

DISCLAIMER

This book is meant for internal use only and is not for public circulation. In no way should any part of this book be reproduced in any shape, form, or manner. It should only be used within the company for the purpose of educating and training.

No statement, graph, illustration, or statistic in this book, shall be used as any type of contractual agreement, nor will it modify or serve as a supplement to any existing contractual agreements between the company, the author, or any member of the company. It is for example and explanation purposes only.

The contents of this book can affect individual commissions; therefore, the information contained within should not be used to gauge past or projected future earnings of individuals.

This book is only intended to serve as a guide to help individuals through the process of building a team. Only licensed insurance agents within the company should speak about products and services offered. All sales are made based on the needs, product sensibility, and financial affordability of the clients.

The strategies presented are based on 25 years of trial-and-error approaches. The information given is based on what typically has worked and what has not. Potential prospects are not required to purchase any products or services of any kind with the intention of becoming an agent.

Despite seeing numerous licensed agents experience highly successful careers using this system; this book is based on individual cases. A number of variables can impact results and income levels: work ethic, work patterns, dedication, persistence, activity levels, and many other factors. All participants achieve different levels, and these levels often change over time. An individual's true results cannot be predicted.

The publisher and author will take no responsibility or liability to any person or entity with respect to any losses or damages caused, or alleged to have been caused – directly or indirectly – by the contents of this book. This book is sold with the understanding that neither the publisher, nor the author is giving legal, accounting, or any other professional services or advice.

The views, thoughts, opinions, and information written in this book are those of the author and do not necessarily express the views and opinions of any other person or the company represented.

ENDORSEMENTS

Tony Garcia
President and CEO,
Foresters Financial

"With Inside the Circle, Andy Albright's passion for helping others succeed shines through. Andy shares what he has learned as an entrepreneur and innovator in successfully growing his business. I have had the pleasure to get to know Andy over the past few years and I believe that he has just scratched the surface of what is possible for his people and his business."

Todd Swenson
Vice President, Special Markets and
Product Development
Columbian Financial Group

"It's truly been a privilege to build and grow both a working relationship and personal friendship with Andy that goes back nearly a decade. Early on, I observed first-hand, Andy's successful approach and vision to mentoring and leading by example. This book outlines Andy's road map of key ingredients to excelling and succeeding."

Dr. Tom Miller
Senior Vice Provost for Academic
Outreach and Entrepreneurship
NC State University

"This book could easily be titled Inside Andy Albright. Anyone who wants to understand Andy, how he thinks, and how he has achieved his remarkable success should read this book. It's an inside look at Andy's core beliefs, his zest for life, family and work, and his passion for helping people improve their lives and achieve their dreams. As a personal friend for years, I can honestly say that Inside the Circle truly personifies the man and his vision."

Jeff Bright
The Alliance Academic Cultural
Adviser

"Inside The Circle' provides everyone wanting to be successful in business as well as life the most vital element: perspective. As Andy would say, 'Get your mind right!'"

Alex Abuyuan
The Alliance, Dayton OH

"Andy's book, 'Inside The Circle' inspires you to keep on keeping on in spite of setbacks and difficulties along the way. If there ever was a reference book written when someone needs that extra push to persevere on the road of life, Andy wrote it with this book. This is one of those books you'll keep at your side with sticky notes and dog ears, I promise you."

Stephen Davies
The Alliance, Arden NC

"So many people aspire to be the best version of themselves but fight the distractions and noise of daily life, which limits their progression and growth. This book is a reminder of why you have to stay focused on personal and professional goals if you want to truly find success."

James Hill
The Alliance, Burlington NC

"With every book Andy writes the vision gets clearer and the tasks ahead of us simpler. This book breaks down what a new agent with The Alliance NEEDS to know into a format that will make sense for everyone no matter what their background. I will be recommending it to EVERY new agent that comes on board with us from here on out."

Adam Katz
The Alliance, Wilmington NC

"Once again Andy Albright has taught the principles that will help me be a more successful businessman as well as a more successful husband, father and friend. 'Inside The Circle' is a book that you won't be able to put down. It is filled with information you can use to help you get to where you want to be in life."

Eric Bellaire
The Alliance, Melbourne FL

"Andy Albright has written another amazing book. He has written two other great books prior to this one, the 8 steps to success and the Millionaire Maker Manual! I believe this one is just as powerful as the other two, if not more powerful. It will give you the THIRST for more, and this book will help you BELIEVE you can walk through that door!"

Paul Roberts
The Alliance, Argyle TX

"When Andy talks about winning the lottery by being born in America where opportunity is limitless, it reminds me that I have the same 24 hours as every other person in the United States. Because I have studied him, I have taken full advantage of what he talks about in this book and use it to create as much success as possible. If you read this book and take action, it will help you light your life on fire."

Chris Long
The Alliance, St. Augustine FL

"Over the last 10 years of working with Andy I have come to realize one of the biggest factors of success in this business is how we communicate. That is why I'm so excited that Andy has come out with this new book as it gives me one more example for me to copy. Andy is a master of using simple strategies to be successful and I am excited to continue to learn from him! Thank you Andy!"

Patrick Connors
The Alliance, Mason OH

"With Inside The Circle, Andy Albright invites us to peek inside HIS circle. Before he asks US to behave, he shows us how HE behaves. How beautiful and precious a gift is that? Now, what will we DO with it?"

Andy Riddle
The Alliance, Jacksonville FL

"This book teaches much of what Andy has helped lead me to over the last 10 years. I wanted to create a career where I could provide a great lifestyle for my family and enjoy spending time with my daughters. This book offers a blueprint of how you can do that, and Andy gives you simple principles to help you improve in all areas of life."

Noelle Lewantowicz
The Alliance, Louisville KY

"Andy Albright has taught me how to keep it simple and focus on the basics. He is not just a talker, Andy walks the talk and shows the way. This book shows how you can use basic principles to expand your vision and horizons in a big way when it comes to being successful. Andy is a great example of a servant leader, who wants to help others succeed."

FOREWORD

Brett David, CEO Prestige Imports - Lamborghini Miami

In 2007, my father, Irv David died unexpectedly and I was faced with a decision that would ultimately decide the path I was going to take in life.

At the age of 19, I had to make a huge decision.

Would I continue the car business he built and continue his legacy or sell immediately as he stated were his wishes in his will? My father started Prestige Imports in 1977 and I made the decision that I wanted to carry the torch.

I can't blame him for thinking that I would not be able to make Prestige Imports work without him. However, I chose to give it a shot. In my mind, it was the best way to honor him.

Continuing his legacy and growing the company is my motivation. It is what drives and motivates me on a daily basis. On my desk, I keep my father's name plate so that I never forget how far I've come and remember that everything I have is because of my father.

When you are running a company in Miami, Fla., you have to be bold, you have to make things happen and you have to stay on your game.

I've been blessed, but I have worked hard to build upon what my father started. I oversee Prestige Imports, which has sold more than $1 billion in sales across all franchises. I've continued to grow and expand and I do not take any of it for granted. Every single day is a new opportunity, and I never want to take it for granted.

The best part of my job is meeting people from around the world and hearing their stories about the journey that afforded them the ability to purchase a Lamborghini or a super sports car, like a Pagani. I know that everyone has trials and tribulations in life and no one is exempt from achieving success without experiencing failures.

Fail fast. Keep trying. Move forward.

I had the pleasure of meeting Andy Albright in 2016, and we are very different, yet very much the same. I meet a lot of people who are in leadership positions, and I can tell you that Andy Albright is one of the most dynamic leaders I've ever met. He's the real deal. If he tells you he is going to do something, then you can count on him making it happen. I love that about him, and I have enjoyed following his career and family since meeting him.

People crave leadership and seek out advice from people they admire and trust. While we can't always have personal, one-on-one time with great leaders, we all can read and learn. Inside The Circle is a way for you to learn from Andy Albright when you don't have the opportunity to speak with him on the phone or meet in person. As you read this book, think of it as you having Andy speaking to you in person!

Through simple, yet tested principles, Andy has put together a plan for you to make choices and decisions in your life that will help you be successful. Please don't take for granted the power of this book, because it can be the catalyst that moves you from where you are now to where you want to be.

When you reach a crossroads in life, it can be scary. When you decide to start a business like Andy did with The Alliance or to carry on a business like I did when my father died, it's a major deal. However, if you have faith, work hard and stay focused; the rewards far outweigh the risk.

Andy loves helping people and he does not view the journey he is on as work. I feel the same way. When you are doing what you love and helping people at the same time, you are doing life. It's not work. We are all in the people business, even if we don't realize it. Andy is a master at connecting with people, and he is doing it for the masses with Inside The Circle.

I'm thankful to be able to call Andy my friend. I believe that after you read this book, you will have greater insight as to Andy's wisdom and how powerful his simple principles can be to where you are headed in life.

Take the contents of Inside The Circle and apply them to your goals and dreams. You will be amazed at how much you can accomplish if you take Andy's word to heart. I wish you great success in all that you do.

Brett David
CEO Prestige Imports – Lamborghini Miami

INTRODUCTION

"For the strength of the Pack is the Wolf, and the strength of the Wolf is the Pack."

Rudyard Kipling

All my life, I have enjoyed being around people. I have always loved getting to know people and have always loved seeing people experience success. As I began to build businesses, I realized that as the **PEOPLE** grow so **GROWS** the **COMPANY**. It sounds simple and corny, but it is the truth. When people are growing, the company is more likely to grow.

There's no one real secret to success. While technology has greatly evolved and will continue to do so at an even faster pace than it is today, the principles to being successful are still pretty much the same.

Here are two facts: (1) You have to work hard and (2) You have to be willing to do things most people aren't willing to do.

If you can focus on those facts alone, your odds of being successful goes up almost infinitely. You also need to find others who are willing to work hard, want to be successful and know what they want in life. You never want to be the smartest person in the room. If you are, then you need to find a different room … a place where you will be challenged. You should always try to surround yourself with others who are in life where you desire to be.

I'm constantly working to spend time around people that are far more successful than me. I realize I'm not done growing and learning. I have to keep striving to get around the best people I can find. The better quality of people you spend your time with, the better quality person you will become. It's a law. It is possible to raise your own bar when you are always surrounded by smarter, more successful people.

My true "Why," our **true mission**, is to **build people**. I am clear that I do not know everything about this process, however, I am committed to continue learning how to improve. I have decided to share many of my personal experiences about building businesses and building people. As a person who wants to expand my own boundaries, I know I need more people growing and more people helping grow people.

As people begin to build a business, they want to know **what is coming** and **what to expect**. I know the best way to find out what to expect is to ask someone who has been there before. Preferably, this is somebody who has been there many times. This person will know their own steps, they will know their own history, they will know the obstacles they faced and they will know the place from which they came.

These people express the life-changing events, explain the miraculous changes that were needed, and will expose the challenges that existed. Through this book, I intend to give you insights so you are better prepared to handle the challenges ahead. In this business, you will have terrible situations, bad situations, good situations, great situations--OK situations-- they all exist. For you to commit to build this business, you must prepare for all situations that are coming at you. We must realize that our business is no bigger than the people that are in it. My intentions are to help grow people, and dedicated individuals that are committed to …

The 8 Core Values of The Alliance

NOTE: These first two values fall into the category of ways The Alliance can **PROVIDE**.

1. Excellence: We pledge to surpass ordinary expectations with distinction and superior quality.

2. Service: We guarantee customer satisfaction by providing assurances that every associate will go the extra mile.

NOTE: These next three values are great examples of how we **PRACTICE** what we preach.

3. Integrity: We mandate that everything we do is ethical, honest and transparent.

4. Accountability: We stand by our performance and openly accept responsibility for our actions and reactions.

5. Respect: We promote an environment where every associate is courteous, helpful and diversity is valued.

NOTE: The final three are values that we use to promote our beliefs to the world. In summary, these values are three ways in which we behave and take our core values very seriously.

6. Compassion: We display urgency when dealing with customer distress and advocate empathy for our fellow associates.

7. Community: We foster a culture of integration and shared emotional connection among our associates.

8. Gratitude: We remember where we come from and take time to be appreciative of the gifts that have been bestowed upon us.

Beyond those eight core values, I want to associate with people that believe in … **P.I.E. (Prosperity, Inspiration and Eternity)**

Prosperity: Financial success for family, friends and people like us

Inspiration: Traveling together enjoying all God's creation and giving to charities and non-profit organizations.

Eternity: For us and our friends to have the faith that leads to an eternal life. When this life ends, we want people to be rewarded by hearing the words, "Well done, good and faithful servant." Matthew 25:21 (King James Version)

Beyond the PIE, relationships are a bonus for us.

Relationships: By relationships, we mean people who share our values and beliefs.

AND THIS IS BIG ... they see the Light of **D.A.E.**

Duplication – Copy those people getting great results and those getting positive results

Association – Sacrifice and invest in getting around those we aspire to copy

Edification – Expand and amplify great qualities in our teammates

We follow the actions of those who are doing the right things. We are what we do! Sell, Recruit and Build: We DO the DO!!!

CHAPTER

1

"When you have a dream that you can't let go of, trust your instincts and pursue it. But remember: real dreams take work, they take patience and sometimes they require you to dig down very deep. Be sure you're willing to do that."

- Harvey Mackay

Ladies And Gentlemen ... Start YOUR Dreams!

As I try to describe where I was when I began this journey, I take you to a wooded area with a fire blazing. It's about 15-feet wide. The flames are four-feet high. It's red, orange and blue, and it's crackling ... burning hot!

Then, a big torrential storm comes and the fire appears to be extinguished ... at least you think it is.

But, down under the pine needles and the undergrowth, there's a couple of sparks that are still burning. The sun comes out and bakes the surface of the forest, a light breeze comes along and it just starts to glow. Eventually, the fire starts to roar again. It's just incredible as it burns and starts to spread out. The boundaries of the fire start to expand and it is moving.

Then, BOOM!

Another storm makes an appearance. My goodness. It was getting up there, going strong and then a giant storm rolls in and brings the rains. It looks like the fire is gone, put out for good. Now, it is almost completely out. But, still down underneath there is smoke, just a couple puffs still fighting to keep the fire going. It starts to rumble again, things dry out and the fire is back again.

For a lot of my life I have felt like the fire that isn't

extinguished and it isn't ready to ablaze either.

There were times when I would think I had something going. I'd start the fire, fan the flames and have it burning. Then, something would come along and burn me out. I went into the textile industry after I graduated from North Carolina State University and I thought I had a great job where I could move right up, but something happened. I didn't have the proper credentials, didn't have the right background, didn't have the "inheritable" names or whatever. I just ended up getting doused with water and my fire would seemingly be put out.

Then, I got involved in a network marketing business and I was so excited that I was blazing. There was just something missing. There were aspects that just didn't fulfill me in what I needed. Boom! There I went crashing down again. When I found the insurance industry, I wasn't in debt. I was very happy, but I didn't have any money. I didn't feel like I was fulfilling my purpose in life. As The Alliance started forming, I knew I had found something that had the missing elements I wanted. The fire once again began to roar, and the flames are still burning hot today.

Here I was with not much money, making money daily just to pay the bills and keeping my budget extremely low when I walked into the opportunity that insurance provided for The Alliance. I was so fired up.

I was F.A.T. Faithful, Available and Teachable.

This is not a complicated concept. I was open to doing anything and everything I needed to do to become successful. When I saw that all I had to do was follow and execute very basic behaviors consistently, then I was "all in" and I was ready to do it "all the time." My hope for you is that you are in a position where you are F.A.T.

Faith + Work =Action

What does it mean to be F.A.T.?

Faithful: Being faithful means you take action *before knowing all the details*. Having faith is great, but faith must be backed by *action*. Having faith and taking action will lead to success.

"For as the body without the spirit is dead, so faith without works is dead also."
James 2:26 (King James Version)

4

Available: Being available means you are in a position in life where you can take action. Your finances and family are in a position that allows you to start. Simply put, you can do it RIGHT NOW! I trust motion, I see results and I believe!

"If God only used perfect people, nothing would get done. God will use anybody if you're available."
Rick Warren

Teachable: God works with imperfect people because we all know that nobody is perfect. What great news!!! God does not call upon "the fixed," he calls and then he fixes while they "Do the Do." Being teachable means you accept coaching. You WANT TO know how to thrive, and you change what you do wrong FAST to make it work.

"It's what you learn after you know it all that counts."
John Wooden

I was also R.W.A. — Ready, Willing and Able.
If it meant me getting closer to my goals and dreams, then I was going to do it. It couldn't happen fast enough. I was ready to change so I could see and do the things I grew up dreaming about. I wanted to provide things for my family that I knew they dreamed of having. I was ready to change my circumstances. I was more than willing to do what was needed and I was certainly more than capable.

5

NOTE: In other words, work fast to reduce what you are doing wrong and increase what you are doing right.

What does it mean to be R.W.A.?

Ready: When discussing what it means to be ready, it's simple. The operative word is NOW. Be prepared to move NOW, not later. If you ask yourself if you are ready, in your mind, you should know immediately. If you waiver at all, then you are not ready. I had no doubt in my mind that I was ready.

"All things are ready, if our mind be so."
William Shakespeare, Henry V

Willing: I have two hands on my watch. The little hand says "NOW" and the longer, bigger hand says "RIGHT NOW." The operative word is self-motivated, moving on my own accord. No one had to coerce me. I was willing, more than willing, to do whatever was asked of me to change where I was in life for the better. I knew I was not going to go backward. I was willing to move forward and move fast. One of the best examples of a person who is "willing" I can think of is actor Will Smith.

Smith has often said he's willing to die on a treadmill

because he knows that might be what it takes to be successful. He is not afraid of hard work and effort. "I'd rather be with someone who does a horrible job, but gives 110 percent than with someone who does a good job and gives 60 percent," Smith said.

If you are willing, you should have a similar mindset. You cannot enjoy the extraordinary by only doing the ordinary.

"If you are not willing to risk the unusual, you will have to settle for the ordinary."
Jim Rohn

Able: This is a person who is trained on the basics of life and at the point of learning and doing new actions to move ahead. Being able means you are going to try new things and not worry as you move forward. Your comfort zone isn't going to hold you back.

"Go as far as you can see; when you get there, you'll be able to see farther."
J.P. Morgan

NOTE: Not everyone is F.A.T. or R.W.A. immediately. Some need time to get ready and that is OK. Give them time. Reward and invest in people that are doing the "most things" that show they are F.A.T. and R.W.A. You can do it. I promise, it is in **YOU**! We need to get it out of you for the world to see.

I think everyone has that ember burning inside them. That
dream is in them. I know that desire was put in them by
something greater than them. When I was a kid, I always
wanted to have the resources, the cash, and the solutions to
help people. I wanted to see people do better in their own
lives, and have anything they wanted if they were willing
to work for it. For some people, those things are better
homes, better cars and luxury items. For others, it is about
providing better lives for their families. For others, it is
charities or leaving a legacy. The bottom line: I wanted to
succeed, I wanted other people to succeed, and I wanted to
work with people that wanted to help others succeed.

As a child, our family took long driving trips and would stay
at modest hotels. I always wondered what it would be like
to fly somewhere and stay first class. I knew in my heart
that there was something better, and I know in my heart
there is something better for you. I know it!

What excuses do some people have? I joke about putting
your excuse on a yellow sticky note and sticking it to your
forehead. I don't want anyone to have an excuse, but here
I will discuss some excuses that people bring up that nearly
extinguish or smother their "ember." We just need to fan
these embers to get a fire started within them.

What are you "BUSY" doing? Do What Matters!

NOT ENOUGH TIME

People are always busy. Successful people are busy. Broke people are busy. People somewhere in between are busy. The key to moving from where you are to where you want to be is by seriously looking at what you are "busy" doing. If you are busy doing the wrong things, I have great news for you! You can change your future by 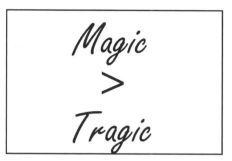 what you start doing today. If you decide right now to stop doing THAT (the wrong stuff) and start doing THIS (the right stuff) then you will see your life change for the better.

Why would you waste time being busy on tasks that don't help you achieve your goals and dreams? People that aren't successful and aren't happy with where they are in life will offer up every possible excuse instead of simply changing what they are **doing** (the wrong stuff).

We all get **24 hours a day** to decide what we are going to do. Yes, you need a little sleep, some food and a few other basic necessities, but what separates the successful from the rest of the pack is being dogged in **doing what matters**. We are all guilty of getting sucked in by time wasters. There are times when we procrastinate. Our excuse for procrastination doesn't matter, changing our behavior does.

24 Hours: What will you spend your time on today?

If we don't change how we spend our days now, then we will surely waste weeks, months and years over the course of our lifetime. Before you know it, the years have gone by and what have we accomplished? I don't want to ever look back and say I didn't do all that I could. I'm going to let my fire burn big and bright. I'm going to let my embers help others ignite the fire they have inside them to succeed. When I look back at my life's work, I'm going to know that I made an impact and that I made a difference.

When you are busy doing the right things and you are viewed as a successful person, people will say it "magically" happened overnight or you got lucky. The truth, however, is that the magic is in the work ethic and *doing things most people aren't willing to do*. Don't let your legacy be "tragic," but rather do the "magical" activities that allow you to live differently than most people. Do this, and your legacy will be "Magic!"

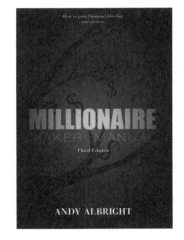

In my second book, *Millionaire Maker Manual*, I wrote that the number one cause of failure in this business is a "lack of time."

In my "green book," which I highly encourage you to read,

I wrote the following:

"You know the 'I can't,' 'I don't have it,' and 'I wish I could' crowd that loves a good excuse? They show up at the office and disappear for a few weeks. They start trying to get their

license, but they never seem to finish. They want to go and set appointments and get into homes, but can only do it once, maybe twice. Maybe they even recruit a handful of people, but something pops up mysteriously that prevents them from working with (a person). It's always something with a *"likes-to-make-excuses guy!"*

My friend and best-selling author Brian Tracy likes to say these people live on a beautiful island in their own minds. It's a place called *"Some Day Isle!"* It's a crowded place, and I don't want you taking up residency there. Be a doer and **NOT A PERMANENT RESIDENT ON "Some Day Isle!"**

I know life gets busy and complicated quickly. That's the reason you have to be extremely disciplined in how you spend your time. Time is the most valuable asset that you have.

Make it a habit to start thinking very deliberately when it comes to your schedule. Before you accept a meeting or take a phone call, ask yourself this question: ***"Is this the most beneficial use of my time right now?"***

Here's some other things to consider when you are scheduling how you use your time each day:

What if I don't go?

What if I do go?

Is what I'm doing of value to me? Is what I am doing of value to my family?

Is this important enough for me to spend time in this area?

Am I working with the right people?

What's the best and worst thing that will result from this action?

Will this small action I'm about to take add a little bit to my future or will it detract from my future?

Make it a habit of having the mindset of using your time wisely. There is not anymore time being added to a day -- 24 hours. Use it wisely -- everyday.

Life is faster than any of us realize. When it's all said and done, I want you to be able to tell people you lived it to the fullest. Some people figure this out and others do not. It's a lot more fun to be in the game than watching it on television from your living room.

I had to work hard to change my thinking many years ago. I reassessed what was really important, and it has made a huge difference in my life.

I had to change what I was doing and I made the decision to break the cycle I was in.

There was a time when if you wanted to find me on a Saturday morning, the golf course was a sure bet. I was never going to become a professional golfer, and I certainly wasn't good enough to even make a living chasing a white ball.

On top of that, I was hanging around some people that, looking back, were not the greatest people for me to associate with. Don't get me wrong, they were good guys and we had a lot of fun. I, however, realized I was never going to reach my full potential by spending my Saturdays with this crowd. I still play golf now, but rarely do I play on a weekend and I no longer have a membership at a country club.

Andy and Jane Albright playing golf at Cana Bay Palace Club

I tend to play golf now in world-class places like Augusta, Pinehurst, Pebble Beach, Bay Hill and far out places like

Fiji, the Bahamas and Ireland. I think the trade off from golf on Saturdays at the local country club to playing golf all over the world was a great decision on my part.

When you break the cycle you are in, it is difficult. You have to keep telling yourself that you know it's the best thing to do because it will pay off for you and the people you care about most. Maybe it will help you if you think about your spouse or your children when you start to do something that will not yield you a great outcome. Maybe there's a nice item you'd like to buy, and that will motivate you to change your behavior. ***Find something that motivates you to change and focus on that.***

Why would you delay something important for something that isn't, when you know it will pay off down the road? Stop it!

Why wouldn't you go "all in" to make sure your family gets to do all the things you never did growing up, that they get all the toys and cool stuff you never had when you were younger, and that they experience life from a view that you only dreamed of as a child. Going "all in" can change those childhood dreams with adult realities.

Don't ever talk yourself into believing that you are too busy to chase your dreams!

I want to repeat that getting what you want will not be easy. It will require effort and hard work. Your results will likely be in direct proportion to the effort you exert as well.

Do yourself a favor and fully commit now. If you are willing to pour a little gasoline on the fire, then your flame will be bigger sooner. Don't back away from your goal. Fuel the fire! Pour the gas on ... NOW!

Nothing great was ever achieved by just punching the clock Monday through Friday from 8 a.m. until 5 p.m. The top people in any occupation got there by working hard, doing things that others weren't willing to do and by never quitting. Be what I like to call an "all the time person" or a "100 percenter."

When you are looking for the "100 percenter" or the "all timer," you have to find people that want something very badly. They want to be successful so much that they are willing to fight, scratch and claw to get it. These are people that want to be successful so bad you can see it burning in their eyes and their hearts. You can feel it when they speak because there is passion behind their words and you can see the commitment in their actions. You can clearly see that they are "all in" when they are working with new people and clients.

Those are the people I want to spend my time around. That's the kind of people I want on my team.

15

I want you to realize that you can't do anything in life without time. You have to remind yourself that you do have the time, but you have to make the time to get things done. You have a lot of time. And, the best time to do something is RIGHT NOW! :-)

It's that effort and mindset that will take you to the top. Can you make that effort? Are you willing to do the *little things* to get there?

Now

>

Later

If you started working on something right now, you'd be far closer to being there than you ever will if you never move!

I've never finished a book I didn't open and start reading. BUT, I've finished many books by taking 15 minutes a day to read every day for two weeks.

I've never jogged a mile when I didn't put one foot in front of the other. BUT, I've jogged many miles – painfully I'm afraid to say – when I got out of bed, tied my shoes and headed out the door.

I've never talked to somebody on the phone without picking up the phone. BUT, I've talked to thousands upon thousands of people because I picked up the phone and started making dials.

I've never completed anything I didn't start. BUT, over the years I've completed many tasks others did not and never will, because I moved. I started. I persisted. I never gave up.

I MOVEd, STARTed, and PERSISTed.

When you decide your goal is important enough to get started, then you will see progress and improvement. Get in the habit of doing things IMMEDIATELY. Make today the point in your life where you decide that every second matters and the time for making excuses has passed. RIGHT NOW, you are as old as you've ever been, but you are also as young as you will ever be.

CHANGE LIVES BY CHANGING YOU

How can you change the lives of others when you haven't changed your own life? When you do it for yourself – the most important person you know – then it will be infinitely easier for you to help others do the same.

My life changed many years ago when I decided that I was not going to work in that textile factory anymore. I decided I was going to chase my dreams and help others do the same. There's no reason you can't improve your situation.

Why not help others as you grow and improve? Learn to be a winner, and be that person that makes a difference to others along the way.

There are many ways you can start making a difference. The key is that you decide to improve, be willing to "move" or do something about it, use the system that is in place and go do the work.

Our Alliance Activity book clearly shows everyone has the same amount of time in a day. We simply need to move from Waste of Time Activities (WTA) to Income Producing Activities (IPA), or maybe we should call them Dream Producing Activities (DPA). There are so many things that tie people up and we must unleash the power inside of these individuals by using the Activity book to put people on the right activities that will get them closer to their dream. The only other activities should be Life Sustaining Activities (LSA). All this is for people that want it BIG and want it NOW!

I DON'T HAVE ENOUGH MONEY

Money is very elusive. There is no doubt about it. People make it. They go into debt, and they can't figure out how to get out of it. They copy "the Joneses" or the people that live near them because they want to have the things they have, even if they don't have the money to afford that lifestyle. They don't stop to think that maybe the people with the nicer things are completely in debt, stressed out and wishing they hadn't gone into debt.

We don't want to disappoint our family by not giving them what they "deserve." We try to take the vacations that everybody else takes, we try to buy things before it needs to be purchased and we worry about the vehicles we drive perhaps maybe more than our home where our family lives. There are changes in jobs, changes in compensation and most people plan more for a vacation than they do for their financial future. They live paycheck to paycheck. Now, that person is out of time and money. When you are out of time and money, the mental drain is amplified, and often times it leads to misery. When it comes to being broke and broken, misery certainly seems to love company. *If all we have in our pockets is change, then it is time to make changes* in our daily routines, our habits and our decision making.

THE MOTIVATION MYTH

We are who we associate with, and these days it seems like most people lack motivation. They talk casually about traveling to different parts of the world. They joke about having nicer cars and they are not serious about it. Everybody says "it is what it is." They basically mean things never will change for them. Be careful associating with people who think that way.

There doesn't seem to be that burn in a lot of people around us. Motivation is needed. People that don't have it struggle to change their circumstances. You have to figure out what drives you toward your dreams, goals and success in life. What is it that motivates you? Do you know?

MEDIOCRE LIFE

We settle for what is given to us and we end up accepting status quo. Why do we lose our ambition? Why do we lose our courage? Why do we have to think of every possible bad thing that could happen? Why do we have to put all the bad out front? It stops us from taking a chance. It makes us focus on safe. Why do we focus on the average, the normal?

Many people fear their own children could see them as NOT "going for it," or not taking the risk to find greatness. That is the past, and the past does not have to be the future. Indifference is the death of us. There is the hate of being poor and there is the extreme love of wanting to make a difference and being able to live the life of your dreams. **Your past is not and will not be your future.** Your past has no impact on your future.

SEIZE THE DREAM

As we seize control of our lives, we "sees" that our dream

is important too. For most of us, we have always wanted to make our parents happy, always worked hard to get good grades and maybe even worked for people that our parents told us to, because our parents wanted us to help their friends. We live our lives thinking about other people and helping them. We must remember we have a dream also. We have a purpose. We can enjoy happiness. **We need to realize our dream too.**

MIRACLES ARE REAL

When I travel around the world, it still blows my mind when a 747 airplane that weighs 430 tons and is solid steel can take off, leave the ground, and nobody gets scared. That still seems like a miracle to me.

Andy and Jane Albright at a NC State football game

It seems like a miracle to me that I have front row seats at sporting events at every single game. It seems like a miracle to me that my children honor, respect, and believe that my wife, Jane and I are heroes to them in their lives. Every time I host a HotSpot meeting (our weekly meetings where our system is explained), I see eyes that want to believe in the dream. They want to believe in the miracle.

Do you believe in miracles? They are real and they do still happen. **Miracles happen every day.**

Albert Einstein said, "There are only two ways to live your life. One is as though nothing is a miracle. The other is as though everything is a miracle."

THE END IS NEAR

Psychologists tell us that people who address death, who know they are going to die and accept it are higher performers than people who blow off death, say they don't think about it and pretend like it is not going to happen.

The end is going to happen and you, nor I know when. If you only had a couple more minutes to chat with your children or your spouse, what would you say? If you knew you only had an hour to live, who would you like to be sitting there chatting with you on the bench? If you had one day to live, who would you live it with, what would you do? If you had one more trip to take, where would you go? If you had a month to complete one more project, what would it be? If you knew you were going to die at the end of the year, what would you tell your children? What would you want your children to see you doing in your last year?

What would your highest priorities in life be?

If you knew you had five years, what would you do for your children? What would you do for your spouse?

Your friends? How would you set it up? What would you provide? What would the vision be that you cast for them? What would be your legacy?

Many of my friends have a desire to set up a business for their family that continues to create revenue for their families long after they are gone.

The Time is Right Now!

They want to keep the fire burning and keep the drive or dream alive. Life may seem long at times, but soon you and I come to the conclusion that life is but a whiff. It is short. We need to start NOW. The only other time I would consider starting is "RIGHT NOW." Don't take another second for granted. Don't take your dream for granted. Start making it happen <u>NOW</u>!

Is life really about buying another pair of sunglasses, another pair of designer pants, a car, travel, residual income, time with your family, freedom and low stress? Are your dreams massive enough to change your legacy? Look Inside The Circle and start with YOU.

What changes need to happen? How can your habits and actions move you on a different path that allows you the freedom to live a great life? Let's begin today.

YOUR DREAM IS SPECIAL

The dream inside you was put there by something greater than you. Only you can activate it, only you can make it come true, only you can complete the task that is assigned to you. Don't ever forget that and don't let others deter you from reaching for the highest of heights. There will be doubters, there will be haters, and there will be crabs inside the bucket that try to pull you down as you try to escape the bucket. Don't give into it. Stay the course. Stay strong.

START LIVING YOUR DREAM TODAY

The dream is in the journey. The joy is in the dream coming true. The real winning happened along the way. Zig Ziglar said, "if you can help enough people get what they want then you will get what you want."

The dream for me began when I got that first deposit in my checking account from a sale and knew that I had helped someone. The dream became bigger when residual deposits started to drop into the bank account. Yes, it was small but I started my journey and started to see my dream coming true. I had a business developing.

Did I have problems coming at me? Yes. I was the scaredest and I was the most excited I had ever been. I was fired up to fight the challenges, stay the course, do the work and continue the journey. I truly believe the greatest achievement a person can have is helping other people achieve their dreams. What fires me up is a person who seemingly will not quit, igniting other people's fires and dreams. That is my aspiration for you.

"Today, I am so jacked up to help other people begin their dream journey."

Andy Albright

CHAPTER

2

"All our dreams can come true if we have the courage to pursue them."
- Walt Disney

Who Knew It Would Start This BAD?

I can remember when The Alliance was formed in 2002, and we started "opportunity meetings" or what we now call HotSpots around the United States. I remember a lot of people questioning what I was trying to do. However, the dream was real for me and this was part of our journey to keep growing. It was part of how The Alliance was going to evolve and put a system in place to meet people all over the country, each week, on a consistent basis.

Perhaps you have experienced this kind of questioning or "second guessing" as you got started with The Alliance? I think what surprises a new person is the negative attitude of their friends and family. The doubts that enter their mind. They may be thinking thoughts like this …

"Is something wrong with this or is there something wrong with me?"

"Why did they react that way?"

"Why didn't they even want to listen to what I had to offer them?"

As you are meeting and talking to new people, don't get rattled when they throw out comments or question the business. I've heard every comment you can imagine.

"Are you sure it's a real business?"

"Is that a multi-level, network marketing, pyramid scheme?"

"Others have tried it before ... it won't work?"

"Don't do it. You will lose money and friends."

"Don't waste your time. You will spend a lot of time and make no money."

"They just want to sell to you and then forget all about you."

"Who is going to buy from you? You will run out of warm-market people soon."

"I'm busy. I don't have time. I have to spend time with my family."

"Only the top people make any money doing that."

"When you make money, come see me again."

IS IT ME OR THEM?

I believe that most people desire to be good people. I've always tried to follow the "Golden Rule" in life. I make every effort to behave in a manner that doesn't affect my relationships with those close to me. In fact, I go out of my way to make people happy. When I started in this business, the awkward reactions I saw from friends and family were bothersome.

I couldn't understand it. It was disappointing because I was trying to help people.

I was just getting started and the critics seemed to be everywhere. It was like I was trying to build a sand castle too close to the ocean. The tide would come in and wash away my efforts just when I was making progress. I started asking myself, "Is going through this struggle going to be worth it?" All the while -- the embers within me are just waiting to spark!

I had moments of doubt, but I did not quit. I decided that it would be worth going through the struggles, even if other people couldn't see the visions I had for myself and my family.

Some people thought my dreams were crazy, but I didn't care. I had to talk to myself until those negative thoughts I was having were turned into positive thoughts. I had to learn that it didn't matter what other people's opinions were when it came to me providing for my family. I had to do what was best for MY team.

Hey, to be clear, my wife even had moments when she didn't understand what I was doing. A lot of people probably would have quit. I had made the decision that this was going to be the vehicle that took me from broke (no debt) to living the life I dreamed about as a kid.

"I had to learn that it didn't matter what other people's opinions were when it came to me providing for my family."
Andy Albright

I'm certainly not the only person that got those reactions. Most people get the same reactions and treatment from friends and family when attempting something different. They just don't understand. You are just like me in that regard. It doesn't matter what your background is either. I've seen it happen to engineers, coaches, hiring managers, IT professionals, accountants, nurses, teachers, etc. The more I thought about this, I decided that these people – including myself – hadn't done anything wrong. We all were just trying to help people we knew or had just met. I was sharing what I was doing and building. So, if there was nothing wrong with me, then was it the business?

IS IT A BAD BUSINESS?

The insurance business is clear cut. You meet with clients, meet their needs, they give you a check and you get paid once the check clears with the insurance carrier. It is that simple.

I put in countless hours to learn the business and have trained others. Our leaders put in time to train people. People can do something or they can do nothing. It's their choice.

We train, help and work with those who want to learn. We have educational training, a proven system and some of the best life insurance products you can find on earth. I love all of that. It's one of the reasons people join our team in the first place. They can see the value of what we have to offer. It helps them understand financial issues, but it shows them they can create a better financial future.

IS SOMETHING WRONG WITH THEM?

I was mad, not glad — about the naysayers!

I was not laughing, but a funny thing happened over time. I kept pressing on, doing my thing and it was OK. I kept working. I didn't quit. Eventually, some of those same people who thought I was crazy ended up joining me, supporting me or becoming clients. It took me a long time to understand exactly why this happened.

"Those same people who thought I was crazy ended up joining me."
Andy Albright

Looking back, I believe people used an attitude of FEAR to guide their behavior and thoughts in reference to the journey I was on. When you operate this way, it's hard to believe a person can even get out of bed, much less leave home and chase their dreams every day. I don't operate this way. I didn't when I started chasing this dream either. I believe in letting **FAITH NOT FEAR** be my guiding light. You've got to have faith or you shouldn't even take the first step.

Here's how FEAR by those doubters worked against me.

THEORY: **People thought I was making a mistake**

People are skeptics by nature. They have heard about bad deals and scams. They thought there was a chance this was one of them.

REALITY: I was making a decision to change my life. I worked and this business worked. It's hard to argue with results and I eventually got the results that proved that to people.

THEORY: **People thought I would fail**

People thought I'd try this for a little while and then do what most people do: QUIT. I've had all kinds of jobs in my life, but I've had this job the longest! Why would anybody do business with someone who won't last? For whatever reason, people thought I would not stick with it.

REALITY: The Alliance was formed in 2002 and it is

still going strong. I DO NOT see that changing. I had no intentions of quitting, but it took time for people to realize that I was building a stable, profitable business.

THEORY: People have failed at a similar business previously

People don't want to repeat a painful experience. They also let that experience hold them back. Just because somebody fails at something does not mean you will fail. Too many people don't consider the person behind the failure. You can have an amazing idea, but it means nothing without effort and action.

Mark Twain is known for being one of America's greatest storytellers and one of the most quoted people in our nation's history. One of his famous quotes stated, "If a cat sits on a hot stove, that cat won't sit on a hot stove again. That cat won't sit on a cold stove either. That cat just don't like stoves."

The cat Twain was talking about got burned or had a "negative" outcome to his behavior. Because the cat doesn't want to get burned again, he's going to avoid that stove top like it is on fire. It doesn't matter if the stove is hot or cold. To the cat, he's going to steer clear of that area because it led to a painful experience. Human

beings typically learn from painful experiences too.

REALITY: George Santayana famously said, "Those who cannot remember the past are doomed to repeat it." That's a great quote, and WE all should learn from our past, but we should never be afraid to do great things, or touch a cold stove.

Ordinary people achieve extraordinary things daily. I encourage people to take the stance that your past cannot and should not define your current situation nor your future. People can't see the potential and possibilities of an idea because of past experiences, but I knew I was going to win and I worked hard to make sure I succeeded.

"Your past cannot and should not define your current situation nor your future."
Andy Albright

THEORY: **People fear change**

Change is hard. Change is uncomfortable. It's also inevitable. Most people don't like to change and will fight the change to a fault.

REALITY: Most people will not change until they want to change. I was changing and other people didn't like it or understand it. What they couldn't see, or chose not to see, was I was changing for the better. I was reading more to "get my mind right" and I was learning at a fast pace. I made changes in my life, my routine and my circle of influence. I still liked a lot of the people that had changed their thoughts about me, but I had to keep changing.

A mentor of mine told me one time, "People who want to change, change fast. People who do not change, don't want to change."

A NEW DIRECTION

When I was growing up, I was told the way to be successful was through working hard, getting good grades, going to a good college or university and finding a good job when you got out. I did exactly that. I was never afraid of working hard. I married Jane after we finished college, and we both found jobs and moved into a decent house in a nice neighborhood. We both had cars, joined a local country club where we played golf, hung around friends and relatives on weekends. It was pretty much a textbook story. Why would I be looking for more than that?

I wanted to get more out of life than that. I realized I would never be the President and CEO of a textile company because it just wasn't meant to be. I knew my salary also had a ceiling no matter how much money I helped the company make. I was doing the normal things that so many Americans do. I was moving up the corporate ladder that had a last rung -- I would eventually be stopped.

I decided my family was going to be different and live an extraordinary life, not just a normal one. **I MADE SOME CHANGES -- BIG CHANGES!!!** I stopped going to every social event. I stopped playing golf every week. I got off the standard path I was headed down. People started to notice it and questioned why I was doing what I was doing. It's not like I was in a bar or doing something illegal. I was just making conscious decisions about how I spent my time.

People who lack clarity will find ways to discourage you. When you show a level of determination to change your situation for the better, people will tell you it can't be done. The best thing I ever did was start making changes to improve myself. When you keep doing this, people will be inspired to change for the better too. The problem is they will try to hold you back first.

Only after you start achieving your goals and fulfilling your dreams will people support what you are doing. Follow your dreams and don't stop! It's the only way you can get the most out of this life.

"Every single day, in every walk of life, ordinary people do extraordinary things."

N.C. State basketball coach Jim Valvano

A COACH WITH A DREAM

There's a great documentary on the 1983 N.C. State Wolfpack basketball team that chronicles the journey of Coach Jim Valvano, the highly entertaining character that we got to know as Jimmy V.

The Jimmy V Foundation, founded just prior to Valvano passing away at age 47 from cancer on April 28, 1993, has raised more than $150 million to fund cancer research across the United States.

Valvano's team won the NCAA title in 1983, but the journey they had to go down during that magical season is the real story. I was a freshman at N.C. State that season and Valvano is one of my heroes because of the way he lived his life.

I remember that to even make the NCAA tournament, my alma mater had to beat teams like North Carolina and Virginia during the Atlantic Coast Conference tournament — teams they were not "supposed" to beat -- but they did.

To capture the NCAA title, NC State beat heavily-favored Houston in the NCAA championship, when Lorenzo Charles put back an air ball shot by Derrick Whittenburg to win in dramatic fashion at the buzzer.

One of the first things that Valvano did at the beginning

of the 1982-83 season was to tell his players that he had a vision that he was going to win a national championship and this was the team to accomplish the goal.

He believed this so much that he devoted an entire practice to cutting down the nets, which is the tradition for the winning team. Each player gets to snip a piece of the net and the coach gets to make the final cut. Valvano had his players get out a step ladder, grab scissors and take turns cutting a piece of the net. He didn't just do this once. N.C. State did this regularly.

Dereck Whittenburg, Randy Woodson and Andy Albright

The first time they cut the net down, it probably felt odd to the players. The more they did it, the more they got what Valvano was doing. Before you can celebrate the victory and cut the net down, you have to believe it will happen. Valvano planted championship seeds in his players. Valvano believed it and he needed his players to believe too. The Wolfpack did this even though they played in a league that had Michael Jordan at North Carolina and national player of the year Ralph Sampson at Virginia. N.C. State wasn't even figured to be a contender for the ACC title, let alone the NCAA title. After a rough regular season, the Wolfpack won the ACC and went on a magical run in the NCAA tournament as a No. 6 seed. It was one of the greatest college upsets ever.

What once was just a dream for Valvano became reality. It happened because he started with a simple vision of cutting down the nets.

People have a hard time seeing themselves as winners. They don't see how they can make this business work for them. They see others winning and are OK with it, but they have so many little voices in their head that they doubt their own talents and skills. This is a tragedy that I'm working hard to change. I believe that every person has greatness inside them. My job is to help them bring it to the surface and to reap the benefits of that greatness.

I heard things like, "You won't be able to make it!" What people really meant to say was, "I can't do it, so I don't want you to do it!" I learned not to take it personal. You can't. It's not YOU that is the problem. It's about THEIR outlook, their perceptions and their lack of confidence, NOT YOURS.

Knowing this gives you peace of mind and I'm compassionate toward people with this mindset because I know there is so much more they can accomplish if they would just believe.

JUST CHANGE

The ability to change is magical. It's like a special power that only special people are able to use. It's really not a special power, but it is because so few embrace the act of change! People hate, hate, hate change. They absolutely hate it! It makes them freak out.

Here's the key: WITHOUT CHANGE, THERE IS NO PROGRESS … EVER!!!

We all know a guy or gal that likes to talk about the "glory days." They were the star of the high school football team or basketball team that won the championship 10, 20 or 30 years ago. They were on top of the world … in their minds.

Change is Good

The problem with these people is that life peaked then and they've never been able to recapture that success since high school. They still wear their old letter jacket, go to the high school games, and don't focus on winning in the present or future. The day your past is more exciting than the possibilities of your future, you are simply dying.

People like to rest on their past achievement. The problem here is that success is never obtained. It's not a trophy, a medal, or a plaque on the wall. No, success is merely rented. The problem for most people is that the rent to have success is due daily. You can't pay rent if you aren't working for it all the time. It's not a race. It's a marathon that never ends … if you want to be among the best at what you do.

Why can't people change when the world changes constantly, with or without us? The world is not going to stop changing and you shouldn't either.

Change is an amazing talent. For years, The Alliance has changed. We keep working to make changes that make our system succeed better. Here comes the fun part. People actually "butt" me like a goat on this subject. They "but" me all the time.

"But Andy, you are successful," the naysayers squawk. "Why would you go and mess up a good thing?" How about this: I can be more successful if I am willing to change and make changes that are needed!!!

People actually "butt" "but" me on this subject.
Andy Albright

I change because my heart knows it is the right thing to do. If you want to stay the same, then you will never see different results. You are exactly where you are going to be. I choose to take action before it is urgent and required.

The next time you are outside, stop and look around.

Stoplights turn green and people hit the gas. They are moving and changing their surroundings just by pushing a gas pedal.

When you leave your house in the morning the sun could be shining bright. In rolls clouds and a rainstorm changes your environment.

Plant some flowers, water them correctly and what happens? Flowers bloom.

Life is all about change. It's how we know that we are alive. When you stop changing and stop growing, it might as well be over. Keep moving and we know you are alive. Don't waste today in the past. Life will be boring if you do that. Challenge yourself. Challenge others. Don't waste the life you have. Make the most of the opportunity you have to do great things.

CHAPTER

3

"The only thing worse than being blind is having sight but no vision."
- Helen Keller

Unique Model Solves Situation

After years of pushing to make changes in my life and in the various businesses I was involved in, it finally occurred to me that I had the vehicle in front of me to transform my family's life and the lives of others.

Now, it didn't happen overnight. It took me trying everything I could think of and spending long days and nights holed up in my basement scratching out ideas on white sheets of paper. It

Andy Albright "whitesheeting"

was all that "whitesheeting" as I like to call it that led to the birth of The Alliance in 2002.

Starting a new business can be a daunting task. There were moments where I wasn't sure how big it would be or if we would even be around today, but I blocked those thoughts out and kept pressing to make it work. People around me certainly questioned what I was doing, but I didn't care. I was going to build a successful company and it was going to be part of my legacy.

Over the years, a series of promotions were created and implemented to help show people that joined our team how they could earn promotions. As of 2017, we have 16 levels that are a guide for how you can move up in our company. We did this because it created a clear and simple organizational chart that is easy to understand, whether you are a new agent or a veteran manager with The Alliance.

There were some people that wanted to keep things the same as we grew, and I knew we had to be open to change and show them this was best for us to move forward. I knew that we were not going to be a stuffy, old-school insurance company. Our meetings were not going to be boring, filled with pie charts, facts and figures that would put people to sleep. We were going to attract new agents by being different, being fun and being a place where people would feel welcome.

The result was The Alliance as it is known today: We ain't your granddaddy's insurance company! I'd seen other marketing organizations, and I wanted us to be better. Major investments were made in corporate staff, infrastructure and technology to make us who we are today.

Why did I do this?

I saw the world changing … fast. The entire insurance industry needed a makeover, and I knew attracting the best people would mean investing in every possible way so that we stayed on the cutting edge in a fast-paced world that was not going to slow down.

Another major investment was creating an educational

system that would prepare
our agents to be able to
explain how our products
work for clients when
they were meeting in
homes. People appreciate
you explaining how a
product will help them if
you do it in a fun way and
show them how the product will benefit them.

Product resources

The result was Alliance University, a curriculum that
effectively educates our agent force and teaches them how
to show clients the value of the products we offer them.

All of these investments were important cogs in the
machine we've built to succeed in the insurance industry.
We have built a vehicle for success, we just need to find
people who can use all the resources we have to offer to
help families all across the United States.

People in America don't save enough for retirement. Many
are in debt, have loans to pay off for school and mortgages,
credit cards, etc. They are hard-working people that maybe
just need a little help to understand how to change their
situation, or to even get back to broke.

When you spend more than you save, debt becomes
normal life. It doesn't have to be that way and it shouldn't
be that way. Too many people go to work because they
have no choice. I want to help people make sure they never

run out of money before they run out of month!

Even people who have plenty of money make the mistake of putting it into savings accounts that pay little in terms of interest. Others invest in risky propositions or buy stocks based on the recommendations of friends and family, who don't really know what they are talking about.

As life insurance goes, the majority of people don't have enough coverage. Some don't have any at all, which does not make sense to me. I've always believed in life insurance even before I acquired my license. I've seen too many families destroyed because they lacked coverage. When a breadwinner dies without proper coverage, a lot of times the family never recovers.

This is sad to me. It's part of my mission to eliminate this scenario for as many families as possible.

Life insurance is absolutely affordable for most families, and that's why it drives me nuts to hear a person say they don't have any. The cost to cover a family is probably less than what they spend on a lunch or coffee weekly.

Many of the people without coverage don't even realize how affordable insurance can be. We all know a person that lacks insurance, but that can hit the bar for drinks every Friday and Saturday night. We all know a person that can afford to buy a new car and make payments for 60 months, but doesn't bother to buy life insurance. They know how to make those things fit their budget, but they don't know a thing about whole life, term life, universal life or index universal life insurance.

How can you afford a shot at the bar or a brand new car, but not know how to choose an insurance policy that you know you need? It's crazy to me.

DISASTER WAITING TO HAPPEN

People without proper insurance coverage are like a bomb waiting to explode. The fuse is lit, and it is slowly burning down toward detonation. Most people will tell you how important their family is to them, but when you don't have insurance is that really true? You are basically saying I don't need it because I won't die. We know that everybody is going to die. Not making sure  your family will be taken care of before it happens is like planting a bomb that will certainly send shockwaves to your loved ones when you die.

My job is to spread the word so this doesn't happen to your family. I encourage strong, sound investments in the products we sell because I believe in them and have many policies on myself and my family. I know how important they become when they are needed so I practice personal use by buying the very products we sell to our clients.

At a time when so many people need coverage, another interesting thing is happening. The number of insurance agents retiring is not being replaced by new, younger agents. The life insurance industry is shrinking and policy sales are declining as a whole. There are not enough agents to meet with all the clients that need coverage. The Alliance wants to change that trend!

FILLING THE AGENT AND CLIENT VOID

A study from the Bureau of Labor Statistics found that with normal growth and turnover, half of the agent force will be nearing retirement before 2025. There will be a need for 500,000 agents by 2022. If the insurance industry as we used to know it were doing its job, this wouldn't be happening. That's why The Alliance is here. We are here to help fill the void by helping people get the coverage they need and by helping fill the agent void that is growing every year as people reach retirement age.

The old thought was to hire full-time agents to sell insurance. We think that is OK, but we are fine with people who only want to sell insurance on a part-time basis. Your knowledge of insurance isn't a requirement, because we have a team in place that can train you. We have resources for every possible scenario you might face when meeting with a client. Our focus is on teaching people to sell, recruiting new agents and helping find other people who want to sell and recruit new agents. That's what we do: SELL, RECRUIT, BUILD.

We are still in the insurance industry with carriers that have been around seemingly forever. We have a systematic approach to what we do. We still deliver insurance to clients, we meet them at their needs, and we provide great, quality service.

What we have put together since 2002 is a solid business plan, an amazing marketing system and a way for people to "Have Fun, Make Money and Make a Difference!" If that doesn't sound appealing, then we are probably not the right fit for you.

Things have changed a lot since I started working out of my basement, and it's only going to get better as we move forward. I like to say The Alliance is getting "gooder and gooder" from this point on. The future starts today. We are going to keep helping protect families while being compensated for it. We're going to keep having as much fun doing it as possible. We're also going to continue making a difference in a positive way around the globe.

Does that sound like something that interests you? If so, here we go. The potential is limitless for you, and we are ready to blow up like Mount Fuji!!!

CHAPTER

4

"No individual can win a game by himself."
- Pele

Building IS The Ultimate

The whole idea of building your own business and having an entrepreneurial spirit is that you work to build a legacy and it offers you rewards in several ways for many, many years. You work hard, put good people in place to help you and you expect your efforts to reward you in terms of lifestyle, compensation, and rich meaningful relationships.

No person in their right mind would waste energy, emotion, effort, time, money, and resources to build a business if they didn't think it would last for years and years. Time, effort and money are some of the most valuable things a person has, so if you are going to spend those resources then you want to be successful and see a return on your investment.

In the financial industry, most people don't think about building. They think of it as a sales job where you make a sale and get a commission ... a very nice commission. This is a very transactional way to think about what we do, and it's not the ideal way to think about it when you are looking to build a team.

It's fine to know all about the products, commissions, etc., but it's more important to know how to recruit and build a business. Yes, you can make a great living by selling products. However, you can only make so many sales on your own pen.

Building is where you can really maximize your income

potential and make massive amounts of money. Why is it that people don't understand that concept? The highest paid people in the world are paid for getting other people to "move" or make sales. These people are builders, yet most people don't see the potential of recruiting others to make sales with them. Yes, it's true you do not make a dime when you recruit a new person. However, once a recruit makes sales then the commission checks start coming in. Getting people to make sales is awesome, but recruiting new people and training them to make sales is just as important in being successful when building a team.

One key when you are looking to build a strong team is to work hard to establish great relationships from the beginning. There will be times when this is painful because they ask frustrating questions or they are whining about why they aren't closing sales, but you must work with your team to help them get past the whining so you all can start winning.

When you talk on the phone or meet with a teammate in person, you must have clear objectives. Take the time to help them with goal setting and even making their own recruiting dials. Most new recruits get out of the gate slowly, so anything you can do to speed up their progress is only going to increase the likelihood of them sticking with you. The faster an agent gets paid, the more likely they will take your advice and follow the system that's in place.

The return on your time will surprise you. Anybody can make sales occasionally, but building takes more work and effort. The problem with recruiting a team is that it is hard and you will likely have a negative experience at some point. People will quit, never do anything or just bother you in general. The flip side is sales where everything is positive. Thinking about the immediate commission of selling often outweighs the long-term potential of recruiting or building a team for the long haul.

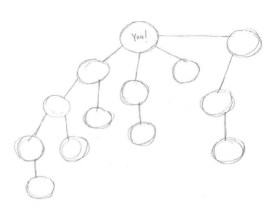

If you think you are building, draw out your team and see how it looks. If the sheet of paper doesn't have other names on it, then you are not building!

Are you being honest with yourself about your building efforts? Do you have as many people as you thought you did that are actually doing anything? Maybe you are not doing everything you should so that people can duplicate you? Make a conscious effort to see if you are on track when it comes to trying to build a team.

Let's talk about a great recruiter. We've all seen a person who brings them in by the dozens, like vultures on a dead deer. I'm talking about a recruiting machine. This person is good on the phone, they motivate others and they do a great job of selling the dream. This person is great in front of a room of people and says all the right things. However, it seems like none of the people they recruit seem to stick around very long.

Why would this happen? It is possible that they are only good at getting people on board and then they don't help the person beyond that. This is more common than people realize.

WHY BUILD?

The reason you want to build is to leave a legacy. You have to know your building efforts will eventually pay off down the road, even if you can't see it immediately. If you knew building for the next year or even five years would pay dividends for the next 30 years would you hesitate to build it big for even one second?

When you were a child did you ever start a project only to realize it was going to be a headache to finish and it might not be exactly what you thought it was before you started? Did your parents make you complete the project even though you didn't want to? If this happened to you, did you feel rewarded once you completed the final product?

Legacy > job

My wife and I just finished remodeling a beautiful cabin 10 minutes away from our home. I can promise you that when the project started, it was hard for many to see the vision we had for the finished home. There were headaches with contractors, builders, landscapers, etc. Mistakes were made and feelings were hurt from time to time. We kept working and building until it became a 6,000 square foot home on 250 acres in what is now a dream setting.

What if we had given up halfway through? We would not be able to enjoy the time, energy and effort it took to build it the right way. The process was never perfect and it took us longer to finish than we expected, but we kept working and making corrections and improvements along the way.

Albright Leadership Cabin

Before   *After*

We are not done with this property, and we are always thinking of new ideas that would make it an even better place for those who spend time at the Albright Leadership Cabin. It is a special place we share with members of The

Alliance, our friends and family.

Think about a home improvement project you dream of completing this year. Think about how and why you want to take on this project.

Why do you want to do it? Is it for you, loved ones, friends, etc.?

Why is now the right time?

Does it need to be smaller or bigger?

How long will it take to finish? What is your ideal time frame from start to finish?

How much will it cost? Can you really afford it?

What about this project have you not thought out?

That's just a short exercise to help you start thinking about building or improving something around your home. You want to weigh everything out before you spend money and time to get started. The project should be a result of your vision, and it's the same logic in building a business. If we could approach recruiting in the same way we look at home improvement, would we all be better builders?

People often ask: Andy, why am I trying to build a business? Let's think about that now.

- You are looking for change in your life

If you are like me, you are not satisfied with where you are right now in life. Maybe you need a career change or just a change in your thinking. People will not change until they are ready. When you a find a person that is ready, look out! They are going to change fast!

- You believe you can be successful

I believe all people can be successful if they work hard at it. People that don't believe they can win never will. That's what separates winners and losers. A winner finds a way to make it happen, even in the face of adversity. A winner is going to work hard to build a team because they recognize the results that come from building it big.

- You have a bigger dream and vision for your life

Did you grow up wanting more than what you saw in your environment? Have you spent most of your life working to find a better way? If you know what you want and talk about it often, you will be more positive and more willing to work for your dream and goals.

- You have an actionable plan

Have you set your goals? Did you write them down? Are you taking action? Once you do this, you know what to do and how to do it, it's just a matter of putting in the time and work needed to achieve your goals.

- You want to build it big

The Alliance has a proven system in place. With your hard work, you can build a team. If you simply duplicate the system then your team will continue to grow. Eventually, you will have a big team that is a direct result of your efforts and will yield what you wanted when you first started recruiting your team.

- You want to make a difference in the world

People will work and fight harder for things they truly believe in. This is especially true when it comes to family and friends. When you are working to make a difference for others you care about, you will run through a wall to make something happen. When we love something or somebody, we will put that cause or person above our own wants.

- Leaving a legacy

Most people dream of leaving behind a legacy of success. People want to know they made a difference in the world. If you are determined to leave a legacy, then your focus on the short-term

Will you Leave a Legacy for others to follow?

and long-term goals will be more intense and intentional. You will spend time in the areas that are most important to you and will help you leave your mark long after you have left this earth.

Regardless of what you are building, you must follow some simple rules to help you become successful and to assure what you've built is right.

1. You have to build it in your head before it can become reality. If you can't see it in your mind, it's going to be hard to ever see it physically happen.

2. Write it down! When you commit to something on paper, you can't help but raise your commitment level to reaching a goal. If you want to be really bold, tell others what the goal is.

3. DO IT! Anybody can talk about it, write it down and dream about it. Are you actually going to do it? Get started NOW! Build NOW! Right NOW!

If you can build a team, you can build a legacy. You are building now because of the payoff you get in the future. Do you see yourself as a builder yet? YOU are a builder. YOU can build a team that allows you to leave a great legacy. Get started NOW!

CHAPTER

5

"Commit yourself to lifelong learning. The most valuable asset you'll ever have is your mind and what you put into it."
- Brian Tracy

YOU Are A Student Of The Business

In this business, we attract a lot of people who say the right things when we interview them. They talk about "doing this thing" and being "fired up" to make a bunch of money.

Then, a funny thing happens. Most of them really want to do this business, but they don't become a student of the business first. They don't make the effort to learn what they need to learn before they get started. They bring whatever background they have previously and try to apply it to what we do. That's one of the major mistakes I see people making.

This isn't Burger King. You can't "have it your way." We have spent more than 15 years working on improving our system so that others can learn it, duplicate it, and experience great success with it.

You can't pick and choose what you like and don't like, and expect it to work. We have a proven system in place and it is in place for a good reason. It works. You can't make it up as you go in our business.

When I see people "freelancing" when they start in our business, it makes me think of a movie that is "older" but has stood the test of time for millions of people. Many of you have probably seen the original "The Karate Kid." If you have not, then you were probably born well after 1984, when it was released.

In the movie, Daniel LaRusso, a high school senior, moves from New Jersey to a neighborhood in Los Angeles. He meets the maintenance man at his apartment, who is a kind, older gentleman named Kesuke Miyagi. Daniel meets an attractive girl at school named Ali, but doesn't realize her ex-boyfriend, Johnny Lawrence, a skilled karate student in the Cobra Kai dojo, is going to attack him with his buddies because he's not ready to let her move on.

After a series of "run ins" with Johnny and his gang, Daniel was more than frustrated and starting thinking negative about his situation. Things reach a boiling point with one more fight between Daniel and his new rivals.

While being attacked, Mr. Miyagi saves the day by disabling Daniel's five attackers all by himself. Daniel asks Miyagi to teach him to fight, but he refuses because he doesn't believe in unnecessary violence. After failing to resolve the conflict by talking to "Cobra Kai" instructor John Kreese, Miyagi tells Daniel he will train him and get him ready to settle the dispute in the All-Valley Karate Tournament.

Instead of going right into actual karate moves at a gym, Miyagi gives his young apprentice physical chores that Daniel sees as free labor for his mentor around his yard and house.

For two months, Miyagi "trains" Daniel at his home.

Miyagi tells Daniel he will train him on one condition: he must do exactly as he says and not question his methods. Miyagi, like The Alliance, relies on a proven system.

Miyagi asked Daniel if he was ready to train? Daniel didn't respond too excitedly, so Miyagi offered up an analogy. If you are walking on the left side of the road or the right side of the road, you will be fine. If you walk down the middle of the road, you will get hit!

"Either you karate do 'yes' or karate do 'no,'" Miyagi says in the movie. "You karate do 'guess so.' Squish!"

Before Daniel-san becomes The Karate Kid, Mr. Miyagi makes him …

Wash all his cars

Then, he waxed the cars

Wax on, right hand. Wax off, left hand.

Sand the floor … right circle, left circle. Right circle, left circle. Breathe in, breathe out. All the floor. Then, Miyagi walked away.

Daniel does circles until after dark, working to finish the deck floor. Daniel says his shoulders are sore. Miyagi says, "good." Daniel leaves wondering why he is doing this manual labor for this crazy old man.

The next day ...

Paint the fence, up ... down – small board left hand, big board right hand ... up, down.

All day he does this until dark.

The next day, Daniel arrives and Miyagi has left a note on door.

It reads, "Paint the house, No up, down! Go side to side."

He returns later that night after fishing and Daniel is not happy. Daniel said he would have gone fishing with him, and Miyagi says you are karate training not fishing. Daniel says bull. Miyagi says, "not everything is as it seems."

To calm his student down, Miyagi takes him through each chore and task he has learned. As Daniel does the motions, Miyagi shows him how it is actually a karate move. The old man has tricked Daniel to learn karate through hard work.

Wax on, wax off to deflect punches.

Paint the fence – up, down – blocks punches

Side to side – blocks punch

Sand on floor blocks kicks

What if Daniel had quit at that point? He would never

have realized how much karate he had learned without ever throwing a punch. Because he didn't quit, Daniel continued his training.

Miyagi teaches Daniel balance by sending him out in the ocean where the waves pound him as he tries to maintain his balance on one foot. He takes Daniel fishing in a small wooden boat. He tells him to stand on the bow. "Up, down, side, side," Miyagi says as Daniel struggles to keep his balance. Daniel asks, "When am I going to learn how to punch?"

Miyagi explains that balance is more important than punching. Without good balance, he says nothing will be good. Daniel keeps pressing about learning to punch, which annoys Miyagi. He starts shaking boat and tells him, "learn how keep dry" as Daniel goes off the boat and in the water. Miyagi starts laughing hysterically and says, "Daniel-son, you all wet behind ear!"

Daniel is not amused, but continues sticking with Miyagi's seemingly unorthodox karate training.

Finally, Miyagi agrees to teach Daniel how to punch. Miyagi has on the most ridiculous looking catcher's outfit and tells Daniel to punch him in the chest. Daniel throws a less than spectacular punch to start with and Miyagi says, "What's a matter with you, you some kind of girl or something?"

Miyagi tells Daniel that all power comes from using whole body in punch, but tells him to channel all his power into one inch of his fist. He is now beginning to understand Miyagi's strategy to train him up to this point.

Miyagi gives Daniel a karate outfit for his birthday and then takes him outside. Waiting outside are the four cars Daniel washed and waxed when he first started his training. Miyagi tells him to choose which one he wants. He picks an old, yellow convertible and says it's the best gift he's ever received.

Miyagi tells Daniel to remember all the lessons he has shared with him as he prepares for the All-Valley Tournament, but tells him the most important lesson for karate and life is balance.

Finally, it's time for the tournament. Daniel will finally have his shot at settling the score with Johnny and the rest of the Cobra Kai gang.

Daniel reaches the semifinals, but is hurt by one of the goons from Cobra Kai. With only 15 minutes of injury time, Miyagi works his magic hands on the injury. Just before they award Johnny with the trophy, Daniel emerges and takes the karate mat for the championship bout.

Daniel miraculously scores the first two points and is one point from winning. Johnny rallies to tie the score 2-2. The next point wins, and Johnny goes after Daniel's injured leg. Just when it looks like this fight is over, Daniel goes into crane position.

A swift crane kick to Johnny's head wins the match and title for Daniel.

All the lessons Miyagi taught Daniel paid off when he faced obstacles in the tournament. Because of all that preparation, he was able to overcome challenges because he was prepared.

Daniel had his mind and his heart in the right place when he took the karate mat. He realized that karate is fought with your mind and heart, not in your gut or in the color of the belt you obtain from a teacher. Daniel also learned that "teacher say, student do." from Mr. Miyagi.

Like Daniel, successful insurance sales and recruiting starts with getting your mind and heart right. When people truly feel like you care about them and their future, they are more likely to trust you and do business with you.

ARE YOU TEACHABLE?

I can't tell you how many smart, college educated people I've met in the last 15 years. You probably have met people that fall in this category too. They are too smart for their own good. They know it all, and will share with you that they know it all. These are the same people that think they are better than others based on this "education." The truth is they have stopped learning, thus their education is over. I call this the ultimate Learning Disability. They've decided to STOP learning.

People who've stopped learning also tend to readily find reasons, better known as excuses, for why they are afraid to learn something new.

They are living life SCARED!

Yes, I would love to tell you everything I know, but if I do that you will not start for a long time. My goal is to get people started before they know it all. There is plenty that you can learn as you go in this business. I don't want you waiting to get started when I know you can be successful now with very little expertise. Believe me, you are going to be better off by getting out there and messing up instead of waiting to talk to me about what you need to do every step of the way.

I'm actually doing people a favor by letting them get real-life experience, which is far greater than if they just hear me talking about how it works and what they should do. Spending a few days in the field is far more beneficial than months of sitting in classroom training and listening to me. If you want to be a good golfer, you don't just read magazines and watch the Golf Channel. You hit balls, play rounds and work at it until you improve.

People are so resistant to change. I have to remind myself of that all the time. I have to remember that people will change when they are ready. Until then, they fight it. When they are ready to change, and change their future, they change fast. I like working with people that will change quickly. You don't need a degree to sell insurance. You basically need a good attitude, be willing to change, and learn. Be a student of the business.

It's OK if you are well educated. However, don't take the approach that you cannot learn more every day. Educate yourself as you go. Feed your mind with books, listen to audios and talk to people who are where you desire to be constantly. You will learn more doing that than you ever imagined.

BE A WINNER

I love winning. I love seeing other people win too. There's nothing better than seeing a person win that I've helped in some small way. Nobody is perfect. My cousin Marshall Pettigrew says, "Everybody makes mistakes." He says it almost daily.

Everybody makes mistakes

It's those failures that actually fuel the feeling you get from winning. When you get out there and mess up a lot, it makes your successes feel that much better. Remember what you did when you were successful and program your mind and body to continue doing those things. Don't forget what you did wrong either. Try not to repeat those mistakes.

LEARN, LEARN, LEARN SOME MORE!

At our weekly HotSpots meetings around the country, we don't just talk about products and financial information. Why? When was the last time hearing about an insurance product inspired you to do something amazing?

We encourage people to share their success stories, and we give recognition for their successes. People are not afraid to share their mission and dreams for their lives at these meetings. Some might call it a "pep rally" and that's fine. We call it inspiration and motivation. What we are actually doing is helping people learn how to make money. Facts and statistics don't make money. It's our goal to help people that drives us into homes all over the U.S. It's being able to change lives for the better that helps get past fear and act out of faith. It's the dream to take care of our families like we never have before that helps us to keep pushing beyond where we thought we could go to reach our goals.

These meetings are like the show "Cheers." It's the place where everybody knows your name. It's where you can be open and honest with people. Our HotSpots are where you can get help, get inspiration and leave feeling good about where you are going. You can also share when you had a bad week. It happens to the best of us. It's a safe place where everybody is welcome!

Take advantage of the opportunity to have a place where you can go and learn every week. Take advantage of the chance to meet new people, experience different personalities of the business, and continually learn to make the proven system work for you.

Be a good student. Continue to learn and grow! Don't allow yourself to fall into that category of the ultimate learning disability. You can always be better tomorrow than you were today! Part of making sure that happens is that you learn as much as you can and utilize ALL the resources you have at your disposal.

CHAPTER

6

"We follow those who lead not because we have to, but because we want to."
- Simon Sinek

What Is Your WHY?

In Simon Sinek's bestselling book, "Start with Why" he writes the following in the book's preface:

"The discovery of WHY completely changed my view of the world and discovering my own WHY restored my passion to a degree multiple times greater than at any other time in my life. It was such a simple, powerful, and actionable idea, that I shared it with my friends. That's what we do when we find something of value, we share it with the people we love."

When I read that, I was fired up. I started making changes in my life, my business and my circle of influence. The more companies and organizations who learn what their "true North Star" or what their WHY is NOW, the more people there will be fired up about their job and life. They will get more out of life and they will pour into people more than ever before.

My Why is...

The first thing you need to do TODAY, RIGHT NOW, is figure out your WHY and your life will change forever.

When you have a clear, definite WHY then getting out of bed is more fun! You don't see life like most people in the world, who are content to punch a clock, buy a little house, take a vacation once a year and retire by age 70.

Throughout history, there are countless examples of people who had a clear WHY that drove them to do what they did. Many times, these eventual legendary people were misunderstood by others and even chastised for thinking the way they did.

A young, aspiring entrepreneur named Bill believed a device could read traffic tapes and process the data. When Bill and his partner Paul tried to sell the device, it wouldn't even work. The business failed miserably. Later, Bill Gates and Paul Allen started a company named Microsoft that fared a little better.

Growing up, Richard was a pretty bad student. He got bad grades and his standardized test scores were below par. Sir Richard Branson is known for starting Virgin Records and its technological spinoffs.

At age 15, a young man named Jim was forced to drop out of school to support his family. His father was an unemployed musician and their family lived in a van. Jim wanted to be a comedian and his dad drove him to comedy clubs. Today, Jim Carrey is known as one of the best comedic actors of his era.

A young man named George was unable to spell throughout his life and his grammar was terrible. His brother suggested he might make a career by surveying backwoods. George Washington helped shape the United States and served as its first president.

Isaac was a scholar whose ideas didn't hold much weight even among his colleagues. Some of his peers even went as far to call him unstable and insane. At 17, he was about to become a farmer. He was such a bad farmer that his uncle convinced his mother to let him return to Trinity College in Cambridge. Sir Isaac Newton went on to become the greatest scientist ever.

These people didn't care what people said or thought about them. They didn't let others stop them from chasing their dreams. They kept pushing because they had a clear heart and mind. They knew their WHY and chased it relentlessly.

When you figure out your "WHY," your goals, mission, and vision grow massively. When you know your WHY, you will notice that others will listen, follow and trust you. Knowing your WHY is not about telling you what to do or how to do it. Your WHY will tell you what you should do. Your WHY causes you to take action, rather than giving you a step-by-step blueprint.

The greatest leaders in the world made the decision to inspire others instead of using manipulation or power to force action. It's easy to define what you do and how you do it. The golden nugget is found when you clearly know your WHY. When you figure out your WHY, you will have a purpose that is so strong you don't even believe you are working when you are.

If people buy into your WHY, they will then buy into what you do. People love buying from people they believe in, far more than what you are selling.

For some people, the WHY is family. For others, it is financial. Some want to leave a legacy. The key is to figure out exactly what your purpose in this life is.

I'm pretty clear on my WHY. A big piece of my WHY is to help people. I want to inspire people and encourage them in a way that they can live an amazing life that is greater than they dreamed previously. I want my dreams and ambitions to be so large that I can fit thousands of other people's dreams in my world.

What do you want? What are you doing to get it? Why are you in business? WHY are you convinced The Alliance is right for you?

Let's find out your WHY and get you on the path to greatness, to where you inspire others by WHY, HOW and WHAT you do.

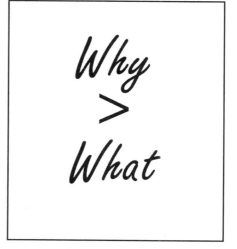

A lot of people think the business you are in matters most. I believe if your WHY is strong, then it doesn't matter if you are selling ice cream,

T-shirts or iPhones. When people get what they want, they will be happy. If that ties into their WHY, their belief in WHAT they do will only be strengthened.

Most people pick a job or business based on the amount of money they can make and also based on how hard they will have to work to get it. People start something and think they will build a team and everything will be just perfect. Far too often, the shock of little hiccups along the way quickly discourages people. If it were that easy, we would all be billionaires.

There are several factors that lead people, who are jumping out of their skin initially about an opportunity, to fall away from a great business plan back to an average life.

Factors that can deter people include: the product is NOT so good it can sell itself.

Oh, man! A person who believes it's about the product is in for a rude awakening.

If all you care about is learning about every single insurance product, you are in trouble. If the first question you have is how much commission do I make, **then you might be in trouble.**

If you think meetings and conference calls are a waste of your "valuable" time, **then you might be in trouble.**

If you don't like to make phone calls, meet people and

spend time in the home of a client, **you might be in trouble.**

If you don't like to recruit new people because it takes time, effort and money, then **we might be in trouble.**

Conversely, the opposite of all those things isn't great news either.

I want to learn everything before I mess something up.

OK, I can sit at home and probably not get hit by a car too! My son, Spencer loves playing ice hockey. We don't have an ice rink in our hometown. That's a challenge.

Do you think that stopped him from buying skates, even though he didn't know how to skate? Nope. He took some bumps along the way and got better every time he skated.

Most teenagers would say there is no ice rink or team here, so I can't play ice hockey. Spencer saw the bigger picture and decided to find a way to play hockey.

Do you think he waited to find the nearest ice rink? No. He got online, found the nearest travel team and signed up to play. For several years, he traveled 45 minutes or longer to practice for an hour in Greensboro. Many nights, he would get home as late as 11 p.m., complete his school assignments and get up like a big boy to go to school the next morning.

Spencer took it to another level in 2015. He could have cruised through his senior year of public high school in North Carolina and continued driving to Greensboro to practice and play hockey for a club team. That would have be fine with me. He saw a much bigger picture for his hockey passion and his education. He convinced me and Jane that he should pack up and finish high school in New Hampshire at Tilton School.

Spencer filled out the application, talked to teachers and coaches and got accepted. All he needed was for us to handle his tuition, which we were more than happy to do because he worked hard to make his goal happen. He even reclassified as a junior so he would have two years of education and hockey at Tilton.

Now, nine months out of the year he is at a school that has an ice rink! He can play hockey every day. He doesn't have to drive to practice anymore. He gets more ice time and plays more games up there than he ever would if he stayed in North Carolina.

"You miss 100 percent of the shots you don't take."
Wayne Gretzky, NHL Hall of Famer and Stanley Cup Champion

What if Wayne Gretzky never took a shot? We never would have known "The Great One" if he was too afraid to try. For 20 seasons, he wowed fans with his skills because he got out there and worked. When he retired in 1999, Gretzky held 61 NHL records. After the 2014 season, he still held 60 NHL records.

Gretzky did have advantages. He grew up in Canada. When Wayne was seven months old, his parents moved into a home with a yard that was flat enough to make an ice rink every winter. By age 2, Wayne was shooting pucks against his siblings.

When his career was over, Gretzky had scored 1,016 goals in the NHL. I promise you that Gretzky didn't make 100 percent of the shots he took in his career. He did, however, miss every single shot he never took.

You can't show up to meetings, and never meet with clients. You can't wait to make phone calls, or you'll never book an appointment with a client. What good is it to know about the products if you are or aren't willing to go help provide the products to clients?

Don't be afraid to mess up!

I tell people to get on the phone and mess up. Get in a client's home and be willing to make mistakes. Keep shooting and you will eventually score. If you aren't willing to shoot, then you will be certain to remain perfect and with zero goals in your career!

Believe it or not, clients will understand that you don't

know everything. Not knowing something is OK, and that is why we have a system in place to help you help clients even if you don't know it all. There is nothing wrong with calling a more experienced person to get the answers to questions you aren't sure of.

That guy is a recruiting machine, but he never sells anything.

Recruiting is an important factor in building a team. However, if you only recruit and never sell anything then why would any of your recruits operate any differently than you? The people on your team will act the way you act and follow what you do. The one thing we do is sell, recruit, and teach people to sell and recruit. We need people who are willing to follow the system, sell, and recruit.

SELL, RECRUIT & BUILD

Recognition Drives The Ego

People love attention and they love being recognized for achievements. It's fun to be on stage enjoying the cheers under the bright lights. What are you doing after the show is over? Are you still working when nobody is watching?

"Don't measure yourself by what you have accomplished ... but by what you should have accomplished with your ability."
John Wooden

People enjoy recognition, but they can easily get discouraged when they don't get the level of recognition they think they deserve. Instead of focusing on the level of recognition you are getting, consider if you have reached your full potential instead. Maybe your desire is to reach a certain level? If you really want that recognition, will you be willing to keep working for it until you get it, or will you stop when you are almost there, but got frustrated? If the recognition is really worth it, don't let your ego get in the way if you hit a rough spot.

Being a full-time, part-timer

Yes, when you own your own business that means you set your own schedule. This is both a gift and a curse for many people. You don't have a boss screaming at you for not being at work on time. Your level of success depends on how you manage your time. When a person only works when they need money, that's a bad sign. Being consistent is the key. If you don't work, how can you call yourself full-time? Don't be a full-time, part-timer. One great way to hold yourself accountable is to find an accountability partner. Compare notes each week with this person and compete with them and as a partner. The only way to get better is to be willing to let your teammates push you farther than you will push yourself.

My Relative Talked Me Into Doing This

If you join any endeavor because of a relative, you might want to make sure it's really a good fit for you. If you don't want this opportunity for yourself, then it probably won't work. Don't do something because your brother said you should. You should have your own path in life, so make sure you are in it for the right reasons and not because you don't want to disappoint a family member.

This is where having a definite WHY is important. If this is not part of your purpose on earth, figure out what your WHY is and use that to find a career path. If your heart is not in something, why would you even want to do it?

If you want a steak for dinner, then you are not going to order chicken. You should feel the same about what you do on a daily basis.

As you are defining your WHY, what and how, simplify things as much as possible. If you know your WHY, then you can work on every aspect of your life. If you are FAT (Faithful, Available, and Teachable) and RWA (Ready, Willing, and Able), then you can take the lid off and be very successful.

In a world that moves at lightning speed, it's easy to get confused and left behind. The people who get ahead are those that know their WHY and use that to guide their behavior, actions and calendar. The people that win know exactly WHY they do what they do and how they do it.

CHAPTER

7

"Thinking will not overcome fear, but action will."
- W. Clement Stone

Ready ... Go!

Why is it so hard to get a person to move when they first start something new?

Is it because they are not processing the task ahead in bite-sized pieces and only see the challenge or OPPORTUNITY as a huge, daunting project?

I've seen people talk themselves into quitting something before they even ATTEMPT to get started. It boggles my mind to think that a person can have that mindset. It is that type of thinking that prevents people from driving to the beach, getting on a plane to fly to a cool resort in another part of the world, or even leaving their driveway in the morning.

When a new person starts with us, I do my best to give them a few things to do to get them moving. The longer they sit idle, the more likely they will quit. Perhaps the most important time for a new person is the first 30 days. If you can help them taste a little success in the first couple weeks, then it is far more likely that they will be around for Day 31 and well beyond.

What we do is not difficult. I repeat ... What WE DO is NOT difficult. You have to be willing to work. You have to talk to people. You have to use your hands to pick up a phone and punch buttons to get people to say, "hello."

Ideally, a new person gets started fast, grows steadily and

doesn't quit. That would be a perfect scenario. What I've found is that we are not perfect and new people are not perfect. Our business has been built with imperfect people doing imperfect things since 2002. The good news is that this imperfection is guided by a system that works — even with imperfect people.

Another critical challenge is to ease the anxiety level for new people. Tell them they are not allowed to get frustrated, and they are not allowed to quit. Frustration and quitting are not an option for being successful.

Create an atmosphere where you keep things positive. Make it an environment where it is a "No Negativity Zone!"

Successful people are willing to do things that unsuccessful people will not. If you quit short of the finish line, you can't win the race. If you never quit, you will win ... that is a fact!

On December 25, 1946 in Pascagoula, Mississippi, James and Mary welcomed a son they named Jim. Soon after, the family moved to Mobile, Alabama. Growing up on Alabama's Gulf Coast helped mold how young Jim viewed the world.

Jim's dad was a military man and hoped his son would be a Jesuit priest or a Naval Academy grad. That was the way his parents perceived it, those were the plans that they had. Jim was a Boy Scout and an altar boy at St. Ignatius Parish, where he graduated in 1964.

Young Jim loved fishing, boating, swimming and surfing. He wasn't exactly interested in his parents' plans for him. He made decent grades and attended Auburn in 1965, where he pledged Sigma Pi. He learned to play guitar from another pledge, because he quickly realized it helped him meet and attract young women. Jim's interest in music and girls didn't help his studies and he soon flunked out of Auburn. His next stop was Pearl River Junior College in Poplarville, Mississippi. It was there that he used music as a tool to earn money to cover his education. He also experienced the music scene in New Orleans for the first time. He kept his grades up and transferred to the University of Southern Mississippi, where he earned a bachelor's degree in history in 1969.

Jim focused on a career as a solo act, but eventually took a job with *Billboard* magazine as a reporter in Nashville, Tennessee. In 1970, Jim left *Billboard* after recording an album titled, *Down to Earth*. It sold less than 400 copies. His label liked him so much, they misplaced the master tape of his second album. This discouraging series of events and his failure to get club dates in Nashville led to him getting a divorce in 1971. Discouraged, Jim moved to Key West, Florida. He worked on a fishing boat and continued playing as much as possible.

In 1973, he signed with ABC-Dunhill Records and recorded a second album, *A White Sports Coat and a Pink Crustacean*. One of the songs on that album was titled, "Come Monday."

Jimmy Buffett had his first hit, but he struggled to find a place in the music world because his sound wasn't country, wasn't pop and wasn't rock. People weren't really sure what his sound was and they dang sure didn't understand his island lifestyle approach to life.

Jimmy didn't quit. His heart and mind was on the music and he was going to make it work.

In 1977, his most popular song, "Margaritaville" climbed to No. 8 on *Billboard*'s charts. His loyal followers, known as "Parrotheads" flocked to see him play, and the 1980s saw Buffett become more of an entrepreneur. He opened the first Margaritaville restaurant in 1987 in Key West, Florida. He invested in a minor league baseball team with actor and comedian Bill Murray. He launched Radio Margaritaville, which can be heard on Sirius satellite radio. He loaned naming rights to Outback Restaurants to open a chain called Cheeseburger in Paradise.

As an author, Jimmy published several books and topped *The New York Times* best-seller list for fiction and non-fiction. He is only one of eight people to achieve this feat along with Ernest Hemingway, John Steinbeck, William Styron, Irving Wallace, Dr. Seuss, Mitch Albom and Glenn Beck.

In 2003, he recorded "It's Five O'clock Somewhere" with Alan Jackson. It earned the duo the *Country Music Award* for Vocal Event, a Grammy nod for Best Country Collaboration with Vocals, and the American Society of

Composers, Authors, and Publishers (ASCAP) Song of the Year. Until that point, he'd never won any major award or been recognized for his music outside of his loyal fan base. After cranking out more than 40 albums since he started, Buffett is still going strong in his late 60s. Most of his albums have reached gold, platinum, or multi-platinum status.

Buffett produced, acted in, and created the soundtrack for the film *Hoot*, based on a children's book released in 2006. He's also made guest appearances on *CBS'* Hawaii 5-0.

Jimmy tours annually, performs benefit concerts for disaster relief, and supports political campaigns. He has opened several resorts and casinos as well. Heck, now he has a new following beyond his "Parrotheads." Their children and grandchildren now follow Buffett and are known as "Parakeets."

What if Jimmy had quit? None of it would have happened for him. The good news is he didn't.

Not a bad run for a guy who failed repeatedly at making it in the music business. Because Jimmy never gave up on his dream, he is one of the most successful artists of his generation. If he had given up, he would not enjoy the amazing life he leads today. He never gave up on his dream because he believed he was going to make it. He had the right attitude and didn't stop before he reached the top. He kept going!

"Quitting doesn't enter my mind."
Jimmy Buffett

People would rather find a reason not to do something than to just do it.

The grass needs mowing, there are dirty dishes in the sink, the laundry keeps piling up and there are bills to pay ... somebody needs to take action. These chores will not just go away without action.

Why do people put off what they can do right now until a later time?

Maybe they are not ready for the change that comes with starting a new business or venture. Maybe they haven't thought out the finances they need to get rolling. Maybe they are not committed. Maybe they are not ready to do the work required to be successful. A true entrepreneur like Jimmy Buffett would not let those excuses stop him from his dream. Be patient with new people, but work with those you believe are willing to do what others are not.

When the newness wears off, will you still be in the game?

You probably remember the excitement of your first couple of dates. Over time, it wears off and you move on, or you become so committed to the person and the relationship grows into a partnership or marriage.

95

Being committed to business is a lot like a relationship. If you want it to be "til death do you part" then you are going to be committed to make it a life-long deal. Your WHY will often keep you focused and help you tackle the day-to-day of your commitment and success.

If we can harness that excitement and enthusiasm into what we are doing in business, then it's easier to do the work and to get others to remain excited about it too. When I get up in the morning, I pop out of bed like I just won the lottery. I did! I was born in America, I'm free and I have the same 24 hours as every other person in the world to complete whatever tasks I set my mind to. We need more people that are committed to learn, press on when things are tough, and build a successful business as big as possible.

If you don't look and act the part, why would anybody follow your lead?

How can you expect people to follow you if you are not doing the very things you want others to do. If you don't believe you are a business person then you won't be. BELIEVE IT!

"Whether you think you can, or you think you can't – you're right."
Henry Ford

Believe you are in business. Put effort in your business like your life depends on it. Be proud of what you do. The manner in which you carry yourself around people will directly impact how successful you are in business. People like confidence in their leaders. If you lack confidence and outwardly have doubts about what you are doing, you better believe that people will pick up on it. The first obstacle in being successful is to convince yourself you can do great things.

Whether you are working part-time or full-time in this business, you need to treat it like YOUR business. If you look around, you will probably notice those who are successful invest heavily in their business. They invest money, time, effort and emotion. It's important to them and it should be to you too if you are invested in your dream.

I understand that you might want to tip toe in the shallow water when you start working with us. However, the faster you get in the water, the sooner you can swim up and down the pool. We've built a system to help you get started fast and I encourage you to take full advantage of all the tools and resources we have in place to help you.

Be proud of what you do and who you are!

When I started working out of my basement with just me, I acted the same way that I do now with hundreds

of employees and multiple offices in Burlington, N.C. I
was serious then because I wanted to have freedoms and
luxuries that I saw others have when I was growing up.
I wanted to be successful and I have worked hard and
been very serious about my business since 2002 when The
Alliance started.

I strategically schedule out my hours, days and weeks in an
effort to make my business as successful as possible. I stick
to my schedule because I know that the most successful
people in the world do the same thing. Know that you
are in business and act like it! Looking and acting the part
makes a difference in the business world and YOU are in
business!

Be Teachable

If you've read my first book "The 8 Steps to Success" then
you probably know that Step 6 is Be Teachable. Are you
open to a person coaching you to improve? If you want to
grow, "things" are not what most are after. They want to
pay their bills and have some money left over. If you want
to change and have success then you need to be teachable.

When you are new, don't be afraid to try things that
successful people may ask you to try. As you learn, you then
will do the same for others. Don't be afraid to engage with
the team. Decide that you are going to be open to trying
new things. Understand that we have worked hard to create
a system that works. Follow our system and teaching until

you question what we say. When you get positive results, you are going to be glad you didn't resist and not listen to our training. The fastest way to get from where you are to where you want to go is by letting people who have had success with the system tell you the direction or steps to take to get rolling in the right direction.

I like to use the phrase, "Act out of faith instead of fear." If you are afraid, you are less likely to take action. Have faith and get to work!

A License to print money?

When I'm recruiting a new person, I encourage them to get their license as fast as possible. There are 24 hours in a day, so you could get your license in the first 48 hours because the class is a 40-hour course. I'd love to just let people start selling, but the government decided you need to be licensed. I know it's a pain, but you gotta do it. You might as well knock it out and move on to the next task.

Before you can make override income, you have to have an insurance license. If you weren't motivated to do it before, now do I have your attention? The key to being able to "print" money is to get your license so that you can start selling insurance and you can build a team of people that

Act out of faith not fear!

can also sell insurance. Before you start making up excuses in your head, I can tell you that I've heard it all since 2002. I've heard most of it twice!

I've also noticed that people who NEVER start the process also never finish. Many others START and FAIL to FINISH. It took me four years to earn a degree from North Carolina State University. I'm glad that I have that piece of paper (I'm not sure where it is), but I'm dadgum ecstatic that I have my insurance license!!! It's been the best way I know of helping others be successful.

Getting your license is the official indicator that you are serious about having a business. Having your insurance license gives you permission to make as much money as you could ever imagine. It can be your pass to live whatever life you dreamed of growing up. Make getting your license a priority. Set the example for others to follow. This is another way you can show that you are serious about business.

SHOW THE WORLD

Think back to your childhood for just a minute. When I was growing up, I loved baseball. I would play it every day for as long as I could and I was passionate about it. I dreamed of being the shortstop for the New York Yankees when I grew up. Of course, not everybody can become Derek Jeter, and I was no Jeter.

As I got older, I realized another thing I love is helping people. It makes me feel good and I see the impact it has on other people's lives. If you can become a master of loving what you do then you can change the world.

Andy Albright playing baseball as a kid.

You have to believe in what you do. You have to believe in it so much that others see your enthusiasm. Nobody can make you love something. It's up to you to put in the work it takes to understand and believe in what we do through life insurance for families across America.

If you can teach yourself all the "ins and outs" then your belief level will skyrocket and others will catch your enthusiasm too. You have to believe in helping families make the right choice for their families.

PROVEN SYSTEM

If you are reading this book, then you have either already started working with us, or you are strongly considering it. You've invested time already, so why not follow our system and listen to the guidance of our leadership team. We've been building and improving what is in place since 2002, and I promise you that we can help you grow yourself and your income. We've been doing this successfully for more than 15 years and the best is yet to come. We are going to continue being successful with you or without. We'd prefer you to join us.

Another important factor in being successful is to make sure your spouse understands what we do. He/She needs to see what a HotSpot meeting looks like. The spouse needs to meet other people in business with us and other spouses that support what we do. Having a supportive spouse gives you more confidence to set about doing the work that will get the results both of you desire.

FINDING 33-10-6-5

People want to feel special, important, recognized, and have fun.

When I was reading "Goals: How to Get Everything You Want — Faster Than You Ever Thought Possible" by Brian Tracy, I started thinking about my goals.

What is your five-year plan? What is your goal?

One of my goals is to reach 10,000 applications submitted each week by April of 2022. To do that, I need to identify 33 key people to help me find 10 more leaders. Those 10 leaders are people who will find six team players that are willing to write five insurance applications each week.

Knowing that is a goal for The Alliance means I have to

keep hiring great staff at our corporate office. We have to keep teaching people the right principles and skills. It is about people skills and performing skills. It is both things. Doing that eliminates confusion and minimizes negativity.

What you want to do five years from now determines what you do right now? Have you really thought about that? What do I need to do right now? Are you calling people to talk about what needs to happen?

This minute, this hour, today ... immediately. Are you believing your five year goal?

Brian Tracy's 12 things needed to make things come true.

1. Have A Desire

2. Believe

3. Write It Down

4. Analyze The Starting Point

5. Determine Why You Want To Excel In This Area

6. Set A Deadline

7. Identify Obstacles

8. Determine Additional Knowledge You'll Need

9. Determine People You'll Need

10. Make A Plan

11. VISUALIZE

12. Never Give Up

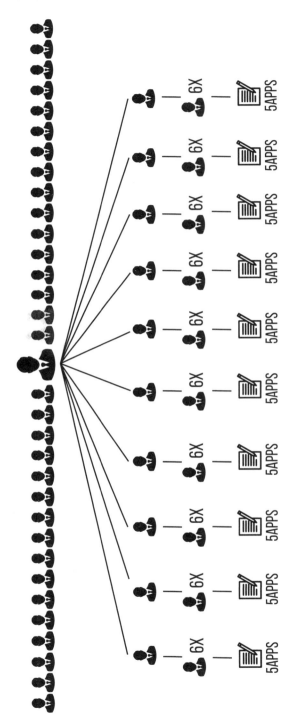

33 PEOPLE FIND
10 PEOPLE THAT FIND 6 PEOPLE THAT ARE
WRITING 5 APPS PER WEEK

33-10-6-5=10,000 APPS!

Keeping those things in mind, ask yourself these questions:

Where are you right now?

Do you have people selling?

Are you selling?

Whatever you say it is, it is. Whatever you decide your goal is, that's it. What do you want? You have to write down exactly what you want (No. 3 on Tracy's list).

I was reading Tracy's book on a flight back from our Midwest Boot Camps, and I started writing down where The Alliance will be in five years. I started getting fired up. I ran some numbers to find out what it would take for us to submit 10,000 applications a week. What I discovered was that I needed to find 33 people that can find 10 people. Those 10 people need to be willing to find six people who can sell five applications per week. Wahooooooo!!! Easy peasy!!!

You are invited to be one of the 33 people I'm looking for. You can be one of those 33 if you decide to do it. It's this simple: Can you find 10 people who can find six people who can write five policies a week? I am interviewing, looking, finding and identifying the people that want to do that NOW!!! (No. 9 on Tracy's list)

How do you become one? You talk to people. You use 20/20 vision by finding people that are selling and recruiting like crazy. They are hiring every week and can't get it off their mind. They are selling applications and finding people to help us recruit and sell with The Alliance.

If you are one of the 33 people, you will make at least a million dollars annually. On the low end, you would be making $160,000 monthly or just north of 1.9 million annually. If you are one of my 33 people, then I am focused on helping you as much as possible during the next five years.

I've set the goal and I'm starting NOW. People need to ask themselves if they are one of the 33. That's the question people need to be asking.

Oh yeah, another one of my goals is helping 12 key people earn $1 million per month by April of 2020!!!

I made a list of all the things I have to do to reach my goal. I need to find leaders, hire more staff, work with accountants, recruit more people, use principles and skills, etc. I've got notes everywhere so that my mind is constantly thinking about getting to 10,000 applications every single week in five years.

Keep in mind that the numbers don't even count the people writing less than five applications per week.

Values, Belief, Expectations, Attitude, and Actions.

Don't wait for the emotion to react. In your life, what does it take to move on all five of those fronts? Do you have to pretend like you are riding a jet ski to get excited? If thinking about that helps you smile, be motivated, etc. then think about riding a jet ski. Find whatever it is that gets you to do the things you need to do. When figure those things out, spend your time focused on doing those things repeatedly. That's what successful people practice daily, and it is why they are the best at what they do.

It starts with writing down your goals. Once it is on paper, you can take action. You are not thinking about the negative, you are thinking about the future and how awesome it's going to be.

Have you memorized The Alliance's 8 Core Values?

How about the 8 Steps to Success?

I should be able to rattle off both those all the time. I need to find people that follow our values and do the 8 Steps.

My 33 people are going to have values that line up with Excellence, Service, Integrity, Accountability, Respect, Compassion, Community and Gratitude.

My 33 are going to understand and actively practice the 8 Steps: Personal Use, Work, Listen, Read, Attend ALL Meetings, Be Teachable, Be Accountable and Communicate With A Positive Attitude.

If you want to earn more, you are going to have to learn more. I'm going to find out who is reading the right books and working hard to improve.

The leaders I'm trying to develop will use many of the principles in the following books:

"The Magic of Thinking Big" by David J. Schwartz

"Goals" by Brian Tracy

"First Things First" by Stephen Covey

"People Factor" by Van Moody

Those four books, along with my 8 Steps and MMM books can serve as the base to help people get on the right track quickly.

In 20 years of hiring people, I have found that more people have quitability than stickability. People will quit something in a second. When you find people that have stickability then you have a winner. How do I do that? You get involved. You hang around the leaders of The Alliance at meetings and events. You associate with people. You talk to everybody you meet. There's a ton of stuff you need to learn. You follow The Alliance Playbook. You memorize it. It's that important.

What if you were playing in a championship game and your quarterback doesn't know the play the coach is telling him to run? If he's serious then he already knows the play and doesn't even hesitate to take action.

Do you know what GS3 is? Quick! If you don't know, find somebody who can teach you about Get Started, Goal

Set, Go Serve. Go watch a video on this topic at www. NAAUniversity.com!!!

Whatever you do will be copied. If you want to be a jerk to people, rest assured people working with you will be jerks to others. If you respect people and treat them correctly, you can bet that they will follow you and be nice to people. People will copy or duplicate you whether you want them to or not. Just like with children, adults set the example. What example are you setting?

My mindset is that I have to get 33 people trained and copying me. I've got to do things the right way because I know I will be copied by others.

I've set the goal of five years but I want to get there faster.

YOU are important. People will copy you so what you do is important. Knowing your job is important, you will set the tone for others. Watch what people do more than what they say. What people say is important, but not if their actions don't line up with their words.

You will behave like the people you spend the most time with. You will pick up mannerisms from those you associate with. Think about children and how fast they pick up on their environment. It starts at an early age and never really stops. People copy people.

It's about eliminating obstacles, helping people by correcting and then you can be rewarded with FUN. When you work hard, you get to have fun as a reward.

People are not born leaders. They have to learn how to lead by watching others who have learned it. It's YOUR job to create the example of selling and recruiting. You are setting the pace. Part of doing that is continuing to learn, teaching people what to do and remind yourself and others what they need to do.

The ideal person is one who sells and recruits with The Alliance. BOFUM is the one thing we do!!!

People need to hear that you believe in them. They need to hear you tell them they have greatness inside them. They need to know you care about them and that you think they matter.

This is not complicated. I'm going to have 33 people that are making multi-million dollar incomes before April of 2019. To reach that goal, I've got to work hard on things that are urgent and important. I can't waste time on meaningless endeavors that erode massive amounts of time. That's my goal and that's what I'm going to do. Read "First Things First" by Stephen Covey to learn about the Four Quadrants – Q1, Q2, Q3 and Q4!!!

I'm going to help people before I need them to help me. I'm going to find bold people that want to win big. I'm going to find people that are doing the basics. I'm going to help people that have set their own goals. I'm committed to following The Alliance playbook. I'm going to follow the "two are better than one" mindset. It's how I'm going to do more for the next five years.

The last 15 years have been unbelievable and I'm grateful for that. However, I just turned 53 and the next five years are going to be even bigger and better. If YOU have the desire and the "want to," then I'm letting you know now ... YOU CAN DO IT!

Who are you looking for? You are looking for people that are Ready, Willing and Able. People that are F.A.T. – Faithful, Available, Teachable.

My name is Andy Albright and I'm going to help YOU be one of the 33 people that help The Alliance reach our 10,000 applications goal before April of 2019. 33-10-6-5 is just the beginning. The Alliance is going to build a legacy and it starts right now.

THE POWER OF HABIT

In Charles Duhigg's book, "The Power of Habit," he writes that it takes roughly 30 days to create or break a habit. If you can stop or START something and stick with it for 30 straight days then you have created a behavior that is likely to keep repeating itself.

How do our brains create habits? According to Duhigg, it boils down to a very simple, three-part loop. There's a **cue**, which triggers your brain to go in automatic mode and begins the habit or action. The routine, which can be physical, mental or emotional, comes next. Finally, the reward comes into play. This final part is what "teaches" or "trains" your brain to remember this or not.

If we can get you started doing the right "habits" from Day 1 then by Day 30 you should have created a routine that will put you on the path to success with us. At the same time, if we can eliminate or correct some "not so good" habits for 30 days, then life will be easier for you too.

Maybe you won't to stop a bad habit, exercise more or greet people with a big smile and handshake. Part of what we do is help people figure out what they want, give them clear instructions on how to get it, and get them started on achieving their goal.

I strongly believe that the first 30 days is critical to making sure a person is headed in the right direction. Our job is to make sure a person is doing what they should be doing early on. In order to do this, we must ask questions and "inspect what we expect." You will only know what you inquire about. Helping people get off to a fast start makes all the difference in the world. People too often make the mistake of saying things like, "it's only 30 days … what can really happen in 30 days?" We must strive to get more and more done in the first 30 days with new people.

Don't make the mistake of thinking it's only 30 days. This amount of time is long enough to change your life forever. You can create great habits and eliminate awful, non-income producing activities.

Make the effort to do the habits NOW that will create the future you have dreamed of NOW.

According to a U.S. census, there were roughly 320 million people in the United States in 2014. If you can find five or six people that follow our system, do the right things we teach and aren't afraid to work hard; your life will never be the same. Doors you didn't even know existed will be opened for you. You will be afforded the chance to see the world. You will be able to buy things you've only heard about or seen on television or in magazines. Before you get caught up in "seeing" the dream, start "seizing it" by doing the work that will allow you to have everything you've ever wanted.

Don't talk about it or merely dream about it. Get your proverbial fishing pole and start casting your line in the water. There's plenty of fish in the pond, but the fish aren't going to jump out on the bank for you.

Do the work, and you'll get the reward!

CHAPTER

8

"I believe that everyone is the keeper of the dream – and by tuning into one another's secret hopes, we can become better friends, better partners, better parents and better lovers."
- **Oprah Winfrey**

Going From 1 To 11 In 1 Step

In my book, "Millionaire Maker Manual," I briefly cover a topic that deserves more attention. The following pages will go more in depth on the subject of how soon a new person should introduce his/her spouse/partner to the business. There is no universal answer to when this should happen, but the sooner the better is an accurate way to answer this question.

Let's look at this from a number of different angles and situations.

When you recruit a new person, the process of building a strong relationship begins. One way to strengthen this is by meeting the spouse … as soon as possible. Inviting the spouse into the discussion early will pay huge dividends down the road for you and the new recruit.

I like to say that statistically speaking a new person and spouse sitting side by side have an 11 times greater possibility for success than if the new recruit was alone.

The excitement level is elevated. The dream level is higher. The "buy in" factor goes through the roof when they are both on the same page.

A husband and wife have a huge impact on the attitude and behavior of each other. When obstacles (or opportunities) come up – and they do – there will be a support system in place where encouragement between the couple will not allow them to fail or accept defeat.

When things look bleak, the spouse can be the reason all is not lost. As long as they both don't give up or quit on the same day, they can work through any problems, and their business will thrive.

Through building with a couple and not an individual, we often see that the spouse is actually the leader. Having a couple on board together doubles your potential network because they have their own "circle of influence," and they bring people from different walks of life than their spouse.

MY FIRST BIG RECRUIT

When I met my wife, Jane, I actually thought she was one of my distant cousins. We were both attending different high schools then, but were the same age. I would see her a few times a year at what I believed were strictly extended family gatherings. My mom informed me that she was NOT my cousin, and that I should call her up to ask her on a date.

Yes! My potential dating pool expanded because Jane Hooks was not my cousin. I knew I had a chance. That was all I needed to know.

Let the recruitment begin. A few phone calls later, we were on our first date.

Jane was my first big recruiting close, and I am so glad my mom made it clear that she was not my cousin because I never would have called her.

Andy and Jane Albright dating during college

I was at North Carolina State in Raleigh, N.C. in textiles school. Jane was in Greensboro, N.C. at the University of North Carolina at Greensboro. We burned up the roads on weekends spending as much time together as we could.

After graduation, we were married and found jobs. I worked at Burlington Industries, a denim factory, and Jane was an eighth-grade school teacher. We were living the American dream ... and we were broke!

We didn't know any better, but I knew that I wanted my family to have more. We had done what our parents, teachers and friends had told us to do growing up and it wasn't working.

We were college graduates when that wasn't all that common and we were struggling. I could see that this was not the vision had for our lives.

The good news?

I was not afraid to work hard to figure out how to change our future. I decided that I was going to do WHATEVER it took for us to make it happen in a big way. The other thing in my favor was that Jane realized that she had to be willing to let me burn up the highway to make it happen. She had to put up with people being at our house … a lot. She didn't always like it and we did argue at times, but she was willing to sacrifice "normal people stuff" so that we could reach the point where we enjoy an extraordinary life. We gave up some of the so-called good things because we believed in our heart that the payoff would be great things … even if we had to wait a little while for that to happen.

It didn't happen overnight, but it started with making small daily changes. If we both didn't agree to be in this together, it is very likely we would not have reached this point in our lives.

If we had both given up at any point, it would not have worked.

Fortunately, neither of us quit at the same time and our business continues to grow to this day. I'm sharing all of this so that you realize just how important it is to have the spouse on board. It makes life easier for everybody.

Examples of How YOU Can Go From 1 to 11 With Your Partner

1. Don't separate work from the rest of your life – use "Off Balance" book by Matthew Kelly to find great examples of this.

2. Learn to integrate work and home - Take advantage of the intense relationship married people have

3. Reap the benefits of being bosses

4. Separate personal subjects from business subjects

5. Be respectful and honest

6. Mutually agree to each other's roles

7. Grow ... together!

8. Have distinct roles and responsibilities

9. Be opposite except in your purpose

10. Success more important than who gets credit

11. Know your spouse is fiercest advocate and toughest critic

12. Get away together

13. Be open to compromise

14. Keep your business out of the bedroom

15. Leverage innumerable benefits

16. Seek third-party advice from those you trust

The National Federation of Independent Business found that 43 percent of small businesses are family-owned businesses. Of those, 53 percent of those identified a spouse as sharing day-to-day management.

There are great examples of couples running successful businesses together like Marion and Mike Ilitch, who own Little Caesar's, the Detroit Tigers, and have operated many businesses together over the years. Mike passed away in 2017, but he leaves behind an amzing legacy for his wife and children to continue.

I met Billy D. Prim and his wife, Debbie at a Winston-Salem Dash minor league baseball game in Winston-Salem, N.C. a few years ago. Prim, who started Blue Rhino propane before selling it for more than $400 million, was open and honest when talking about working and keeping his wife happy at home. Billy, who owns PRIMO Water in addition to the Dash now, believes in working. He doesn't like sitting around.

"I work and do as much as my wife will let me do," Billy told me during that game.

I immediately nodded and told him I understood exactly what he meant. I work at home when I can, but I know that I have to shut down at times to do things with family because that is very important.

When I am engaged in family time, then I do my best to make sure that it is quality time where we get the most out of that time together. If we are not watching a movie or eating together, then I'm probably going to sneak in a few phone calls and emails because that's what I need to be doing.

You can balance work and family, even when you are not at the office. There is too much to do not to use "free time" to complete little things that can be done with little effort.

CHAPTER

9

"Do you want to know who you are? Don't ask. Act! Action will delineate and define you."
- Thomas Jefferson

Right Now

What are you doing RIGHT NOW? Are you sitting on the sidelines watching the game, or are you planning, thinking and taking action to get what you want in life?

In this chapter, I'm going to map out things you can do to act RIGHT NOW. Yes, acrostics can be silly, but if it helps you move and do things that others don't then I'll be silly all day long. Pay close attention to each letter in RIGHT NOW and use the principles to make yourself and others around you better.

Risk vs. Reward Proposition

Ignite the Spark!

Get to Work

Heart to dream big

Take Chances

Never Give Up

Own Your Words and Actions

Win!!!

On July 31, 1958, a boy was born in Pittsburgh, Pennsylvania. He grew up with a typical middle-class childhood. His father worked for almost 50 years in a car upholstery shop. His grandfather emigrated from Russia and sold merchandise to people out of the back of his truck.

It was that grandfather that taught this young man how to make a deal and create a better life for himself. The boy worked hard and at 12 sold sets of garbage bags to save enough money to buy some shoes that he wanted. By high school, the boy named Mark became a stamp and coin salesman.

Mark was a go-getter and this attitude carried over to the classroom. He took classes at the University of Pittsburgh during his junior year and skipped his senior year of high school to enroll full-time in college. After a year at Pitt, Mark transferred to Indiana University.

In an effort to make money to pay tuition, he offered dance lessons to fellow students. As word spread of his talent, Mark was soon hosting parties at the local National Guard armory.

After his graduation in 1981, Mark moved back to Pittsburgh and took a job at a bank that was in the process of switching over to computers. The young man immersed himself in the study of machines and networking. Mark decided to move to Dallas, Texas in 1982.

Mark Cuban scored a job selling software, but soon decided he would be better off starting his own business as a consultant. He became an expert in computers and computer networking. He soon built a profitable company that he sold to CompuServe.

With millions in the bank, Mark could have set back and enjoyed life comfortably. He was just getting started.

Seeing the future of computers and the Internet, Mark and a classmate from Indiana started AudioNet in 1995. The idea came from their shared love of Hoosier basketball. They wanted to listen to the games, but lived too far away to pick up games on the radio. The company grew as word spread and eventually was renamed Broadcast.com. The company went public in 1998 and its stock reached $200 a share. A year later, Mark and his partner sold the company to Yahoo! for a cool $6 billion!!!

In 2000, Mark decided he wanted to own an NBA team. Mark Cuban did just that, paying Ross Perot Jr. $285 million for the Dallas Mavericks. Cuban had been a season ticketholder, but his dream was to own a professional sports team.

The Mavericks, however, were far from a dream franchise. Cuban's first goal was to change it from a loser to a team that other owners would be envious of, fans would flock to and players would love to play for. With Cuban's work ethic and drive, he changed the culture of the team and the roster! He built a new stadium and showered players with amenities other coaches, players and owners couldn't believe.

Instead of sitting in a fancy owner's box at games, Cuban sat courtside with the fans. He handed out his business card with his personal cell phone number on it, and encouraged people to call him and email him with ideas and suggestions. He was the Mavericks most vocal fan and let referees know when he didn't like calls. His outbursts led to more than $2 million in NBA fines.

"Who lives their lives worried about what someone else thinks?" Cuban once told reporters. "Before you guys were writing about me in the sports page, people were calling me crazy in the computer industry. People were calling me crazy in the systems integration industry. People said I was lucky ... The more people think I'm crazy and out of my mind, typically, the better I do."

His passion rubbed off, and the Mavericks made the playoffs in 2001, set a team record for wins in 2002, reached the NBA Finals in 2006 and finally won the NBA title against the Miami Heat in June of 2011.

In 2009, Cuban joined the show "Shark Tank" as a venture capitalist, helping other people put their entrepreneurial ideas in motion, or just buying their companies and ideas. Cuban has billions and could retire in the most lavish of ways, but he continues to work to do more. He launched HDNet, a television channel; competed on "Dancing with the Stars;" has helped produce movies and bought the Landmarks Theatre chain.

What if I told you that when Cuban moved to Dallas,

he was living with five other guys in a three bedroom apartment and was sleeping on the floor because the place only had three beds?

What if I told you that Cuban's 1977 Fiat X19 that he drove to Dallas had holes in the floorboards and needed new oil every 60 miles?

What if I told you the reason Cuban went to Dallas was because he was fired at the bank where he worked in Pittsburgh?

What if I told you Cuban was a bartender at age 25, because he needed more money outside of his computer job to even pay monthly bills?

What if I told you that Cuban got fired again by a CEO who told him not to go pick up a $15,000 commission check for a sale he made to a client? Cuban went to get the check because he said he had earned the check, and what he did with that check is huge!

Cuban says his second firing is what determined his future in business. It made him decide to start his own company so that he would be the boss. At the time, he had little to lose and it was what he wanted to do. He wasn't worried about what people thought. He was worried about his future and what he could do with his God-given talents.

What if Cuban had failed to take action coming out of college? What if he had been afraid to fail? What if Mark

Cuban hadn't been a person that did things RIGHT NOW?

Well, he wouldn't be Mark Cuban, and I wouldn't be telling you a little of his story. Thank God for Cuban and people like him with dreams as big as his. Think like Cuban and take the steps that encourage you to act RIGHT NOW!

Risk vs. Reward Proposition

How many times have you heard somebody tell a young child not to do something because they might get hurt?

How many time have you told somebody that you are about to get on a plane to fly somewhere and they immediately respond by saying, "You be careful getting on those planes!"

What a sad mindset that person has about flying.

Now, these same people that are questioning your behavior will get right in a car and drive down the highway where we know it is undoubtedly more dangerous than flying from airport A to airport B.

A recent article in *USA Today* tackled this subject. The National High Traffic Safety Administration compiles and researches accident statistics for the United States. In 2008, it found that there were 1.27 fatalities per 100 million vehicle miles traveled. That rate was 1.58 per 100 million miles in 1998. Conversely, the National Transportation Safety Board studies aviation accident data. In 2008, it showed that only 20 accidents for U.S. air carriers operating scheduled service. This basically equals ZERO accidents per million flying miles. In other words, nobody died and only five people were seriously injured.

To break it down even further, the National Safety Council did an "odds-of-dying table" in 2008, and reported that the odds of dying in a motor vehicle accident are 1 in 98 for a lifetime. For air and space travel (including private jets!), the odds were 1 in 7,178 in a lifetime.

What people are really saying is that flying feels more dangerous or sounds more dangerous, but I just proved that clearly flying is not more dangerous than driving. Maybe you feel safer driving because you are somewhat in control of the vehicle. Maybe people think that way because of the headlines that are made when a plane crashes. Car crashes happen every day and maybe that leads to people not thinking that much about it because it happens all the time.

In terms of Risk vs. Reward propositions, I'll risk a quick, safer plane ride than trying to drive 10 or 12 hours across the country where thousands of dangerous people can hit me while texting, speeding, drinking alcohol, etc.

Hey, I bet if you don't leave your home today then you will be safer too. How long are you going to do that before you go nuts? To borrow a line from ESPN's Monday Night Countdown team, "C'mon man!"

If you never a take any risks, you are going to live a very

boring, ordinary life. I don't want that for you and I think you know that you were meant to do great things.

There are times when you have to throw caution to the wind and take a leap of faith to do something great. No great person in the history of the world got to be famous, rich, successful, etc. by sitting back and doing nothing.

I want to encourage you to stop thinking so small and be bold. Make up your mind now to take risks that can pay off for you down the road. If you can stop thinking about getting the payoff now, then you can start thinking in terms of being rewarded in bigger ways down the road.

Do you think Henry Ford took risks when he set out to build an automotive empire in Detroit, Michigan?

Do you think he was thinking about what it would ultimately become or do you think he was enjoying the journey trying to figure out how to make the best car he possibly could?

NO!!!

He didn't stop because somebody warned him that it could hurt somebody or that he couldn't possibly be the man that made it happen. He took risks, didn't listen to the naysayers and kept working to make his product better.

Ford didn't quit once he got the Model T rolling, either. He improved production, and rewarded his best employees with great wages for that time. In 1918, half of all cars in

America were Model T's!!!

What was Ford's reward? He made a fortune. He was the best at what he did. He took care of his employees. He established the Ford Foundation to provide funds for research, education and development. He died at 83 in 1947, and is credited with helping build America's economy during the nation's vulnerable early years. What would America be like if Henry Ford was afraid to take risks?

How about Wilbur and Orville Wright? If they didn't take so many risks, they never would have gotten beyond being local bicycle shop owners.

Long before they took that first flight from Kitty Hawk on the coast of North Carolina, the Wright brothers started their own newspaper in 1889. Wilbur edited copy and Orville was the publisher. They also loved bicycles – the latest craze sweeping the U.S. In 1892, the brothers opened a bicycle shop where they fixed and sold their own design of bikes.

The brothers loved all things mechanical and they kept on top of a German aviator named Otto Lilienthal, who died in a glider crash. Even after hearing of his death, the Wrights decided they wanted to fly. They took multiple risks and moved to Kitty Hawk because of its strong winds.

Do you think people thought they were crazy? My guess is absolutely.

They worked to design wings. They studied. They tinkered. They kept working to make it happen. They didn't sit back and wait on somebody else to do it first.

On Dec. 17, 1903, they succeeded in flying the first free, controlled flight of a power-driven, heavier than air plane. For 59 glorious seconds at 852 feet, they were on top of the world.

Shockingly, their success was not met with complete appreciation. The press, and their colleagues and aviation experts, didn't believe they had flown. Because of this, the brothers went on a tour of Europe, proving it to the world. This led to them becoming world famous. Taking all those risks for all those years led to them becoming crazy rich because they sold those planes all over Europe and the U.S.

The Wright brothers didn't listen to people that told them it couldn't be done. They had a vision and a dream. They believed the RISK was more than worth the REWARD long before they even got off the ground.

Seeing it in your mind, writing it on paper and speaking your dreams out loud are important. It's the easiest way to NUDGE yourself toward your goals. Be willing to take risks in life because that's part of the journey. Doing things differently is what separates the ordinary from the extraordinary.

Make the decision today that you are going to take RISKS that will ultimately lead you to where you want to be in life.

Don't listen to people that are satisfied to watch the game. You be the one that gets in the game and runs as hard as you can toward the goal line.

Nothing great can ever be accomplished without taking a risk.

Ignite – find the spark inside you to win

Do you know a person that seemingly has the best life ever? They've got the great job, great house, perfect family, cool car, etc.

Every time you see this person, they are smiling and life appears to be perfect for them. Here's a little secret, their life is every bit as messed up as yours!!! The difference is that they don't show it. It's OK if you don't think you can pull this off, but I have great news. You can live the life you want. All we have to do is IGNITE the spark that is inside you to win!!!

"You can't start a fire without a spark."
Bruce Springsteen

Before you can build a glowing, warm fire you have to get it burning first. You need to start small with a spark that over time grows into a group of flames that can warm everybody standing around it.

My goal is to help you find that initial spark that will eventually IGNITE a fire in you that is big and bright enough for those you encounter to see immediately.

You can help start this process by changing your words, your mannerisms and your behaviors. Instead of using words like these:

But, can't, do not, fail, impossible, loss, mistake, problem, refuse, stop, unable

TRY USING THESE:

Benefit, will, when, success, best, progress, value, improve, complete, work, increase

Those are just a few examples to get you started. The point is to be very aware of the words you use when you talk to yourself and when you speak verbally to people. Words are a dangerous weapon and please do not underestimate the impact they have on people.

When you see a person, are you inviting and happy to see them? If you look unapproachable then you probably are to the person heading in your direction. Make it a point to smile, make eye contact, and extend your right hand when you get close to the person you are about to greet. If you aren't already doing this, you will be shocked at how much differently people will feel about you. By doing this, you will also feel better about YOU too.

Be aware of your posture. Stand up straight, act like you are happy to be where you are and watch how quickly people will respond to you.

Practice in the mirror if you aren't sure how you look when you meet people now. There's an old saying that it takes more effort to frown than smile. There's no real proof behind this, but it feels good so smile! People will like you more and they will almost always smile back.

These are little suggestions to help you start IGNITING the flame that I know is inside you. It will take work and time, so start NOW and get that spark started. Over time, you will forget you are even doing the "little things" that leave a good impression on people when you meet them.

Get to work

This is one of the things most people are not really, really

willing to do.

At a very early age, my father, George instilled a dogged work ethic in me and my younger brother, Alan. It didn't matter if we were chopping wood, priming tobacco, or raking leaves, we worked until the job was finished … and we worked hard!

Andy and George Albright

My dad is no longer with us anymore, but he certainly left his strong belief in a hard day's work with us. I don't really do a lot of yard work these days, so my work comes in the form of getting up early to make dials, meet with people,

Make Work a habit!

and do whatever is on my calendar. I learned from my dad that if you want to get what you want, it will take work.

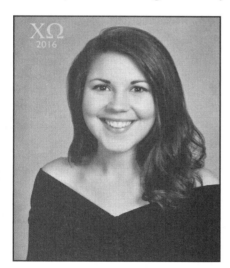

Haleigh Albright as a junior at NC State University

To this day, I've never forgotten my father's work ethic. I've tried to set a similar example for our two children (Haleigh and Spencer) to follow.

Haleigh has worked hard at her studies and she was rewarded by getting into North Carolina State University, where she earned a degree from in 2017. Once she got there, she worked hard and her grades backed that up each semester. Now, she's in graduate school at NC State,

Spencer Albright playing goalie at Tilton School

and she will have to continue to work hard to earn her second degree.

Our son Spencer has worked hard at school and ice hockey and lacrosse. He has been rewarded by winning a national championship in USA Junior Hockey as a goalie and attended the Tilton School in New Hamsphire for high school.

He played football, hockey and lacrosse at Tilton and loved his time there. His next move is to attend NC State, where he was accepted. Now, he was admitted to other schools, but he chose to become a proud member of the Wolfpack, which I'm pretty proud of!

I plan to keep working for many years and I hope that my children will follow my lead that can be traced back to my father when I was young.

Most people will tell you all day long that they are not afraid of working hard. I believe a person until they give me a reason not to. I measure people by their words and their actions. When those two don't line up, then I know what kind of work ethic a person has. Generally, successful people wake up early, put in a lot of work, and don't mind staying up later than the average person. Oh, and one more thing … they do this over and over and over … it's in their DNA and it's part of their schedule and habits.

If you can get in the habit of doing the work, you will be successful. Too many people want to talk about what they can do and never get around to doing it. How about adopting a Get-To-Work mentality? Stop sitting around planning it out. Just do it!!!

Do you think people just get to the top of their profession because they say they want it? They get there because they put in the hours. They do it consistently, day after day. Here's another secret: they keep doing it after they are successful. When you are committed to a goal, are willing to work for as long as it takes and you never give up, you dramatically increase your chances of being successful.

Consider that 15 of the world's richest billionaires grew up poor and WORKED for everything they got.

Howard Schultz (Starbucks) grew up in a housing complex for the poor on the wrong side of the tracks, opposite of people with more resources, money and opportunities.

Ken Langone (Hewlett Packard and Home Depot) grew up as the son of a plumber and cafeteria worker. While at Bucknell University, Langone worked odd jobs to pay tuition and his parents mortgaged their home. I guess they believed in taking the risk, and they knew their son wasn't afraid to work hard.

Oprah Winfrey (HARPO Productions) was born into poverty before becoming the first African American TV correspondent in Nashville, Tenn. at the age of 19. I don't think I have to tell you how her career went from there.

She didn't quit!

Ever heard of John Paul DeJoria? He's worth $4 billion. He created a couple little companies that sell people products they love. Still don't know? He started the John Paul Mitchell Systems hair-care empire and Patron Tequila. He once lived in a foster home and slept in his car.

He didn't quit!

Larry Ellison (Oracle) dropped out of college after his adoptive mother, an aunt he was raised by, died. He worked odd jobs for the next eight years, but founded a little software development company in 1977 that is now one of the largest technology companies in the world.

He didn't quit!

If those five people in the examples I just shared with you had sat around and waited for success to knock on their doors, then none of us would know who they are. They grew up in less than ideal circumstances. They worked hard and made their own breaks. They knew they wanted more than they were given and they set about going after it with great vigor and passion. I doubt they stopped to worry about what people thought about them. After all, they started with very little so what did it matter if they failed to do great things in life. They changed their circumstances in ways most people can't even imagine.

The Heart it takes to dream big

Another key ingredient in the recipe for success is heart. Having the right heart in a number of areas can be the difference maker for you being successful. When you know what you want, you work hard and your heart is in the right place, you can pretty much accomplish anything in this world. Beyond that, you can help others achieve what they want as well.

There are countless stories of people who got extremely close to reaching a goal, but they quit and fall painfully short.

If you were 100 yards from your desired goal and you stopped, how would you feel if found out exactly how close you were the next day? Perhaps even worse, what if another person pushed on after you quit and you were forced to witness the joy and excitement they got from obtaining what you apparently wanted so badly?

When a person gives up or quits, the lasting results can infinitely impact their life forever. That's why it is so important that you DO NOT GIVE UP on your goals.

If people would just keep going and keep their heart in a goal they have set, they would reach the finish line. This is one of the saddest things that can happen to a person who is on the verge of reaching their dreams. If you quit, you can't get there, so why give up? Maybe you didn't want it as badly as you thought? This is why you need to be very clear about what you want, and implement a laser-sharp focus when you set out to reach that goal. If it's not clear to you, then how will you know the best way to attack your goal?

When your heart is fully into your goal, you will push harder to achieve it. You will push harder to make it happen, and you will not be as likely to quit.

When you have a big heart, you are filled with hopes and dreams. I beg you not to let others destroy that heart. Don't let people discourage you from chasing your dreams and goals. Don't let them change your heart if it is in the right place. If you truly desire something, let your heart guide you toward the prize.

When you stumble or hit a road block, let your heart be what helps you get back on track. When you want to stop fighting for something, let your heart push you beyond where you thought you could go and beyond. Your heart can be the deciding factor in whether you succeed or give up.

Having the right heart is about being thoughtful in all that you do. It is about doing what is right when it comes to people you work with, your family and your friends. If you are not genuine to others, you will eventually be caught. Be sincere, be true to who you are. Nobody gets anywhere in this world without the help of others. Remember that, and work on making sure your heart is in the right place.

When your heart is filled with good things, you will grow an abundant mindset and things will suddenly seem to fall into place for you. Another amazing thing will happen when your heart is in the proper place. You will serve others more and they will return the favor. The more you do it, the more it will be given back. It will happen in ways you never imagined and you will want to do even more than you are doing now.

When your heart is on the path to success, this is when you can have the greatest influence on others. You can help more people get what they want because you are operating with giving in mind because you know the reward will come back to you in far greater proportion than you can even imagine. If you can take what is inside your heart and put it in others, then there is nothing you can't accomplish. As you see it start to pay off for others, you will see that it is contagious. Catch the right heart and spread it with others.

Take chances on people who say they want it bad!

A good friend of mine Eric Thomas likes to say, "When you want to be successful as bad as you want to breathe, then you will be successful." I love to ask people, "how bad do they want it?" It doesn't really matter what they want. What matters is this: do they want it so much that they will do what it takes to get it?

Let's say they want to buy a new car. I find out what kind of car they want. I figure out how much money they will need. Once we get all the details figured out, then I work with them on what it will take to get it.

One thing I have gotten good at in the last 20 years is dream building with a person. Now, if all they do is dream, then we have a problem. I will help a person as long as I can see them moving toward a goal they set. I will take chances on a person that can look me in the eye and tell me, "this is what I want and I am willing to work as hard as needed to get it."

I'm fired up just thinking about it now. When a person is

hungry, has a burning desire in their belly and doesn't mind working hard to get what they want … it makes me want to jump out of my skin. Ding, ding, ding!!! We've got a winner over here ladies and gentlemen.

I'm always going to do more for the person that has this mindset than I am a person who is not really excited about what they are trying to do.

One easy way to gauge how badly a person wants something is to give them several tasks. If they complete these tasks quickly and come back asking what to do next, then I load them up again. They are moving toward the goal you've helped them set without thinking too much about it. Keep them moving toward the goal until you get an objection. If you get no objections, they will reach their goal over time. The people that want to succeed will show you through their actions.

I will never deny a person that clearly shows me they want something bad enough that they are willing to give up "unimportant" things to reach that goal or dream. I don't have endless time to spend with them, but I will make every effort to help them get what they want when they show me the desire is there, the work ethic is there, and their heart is fully in it.

People like this will always come out on top in life. It might not happen overnight, but it will happen. I've seen it repeatedly in the last 20 years. Winners separate themselves over time.

"Don't ever give up, don't ever give up!"
Jimmy Valvano

Never Give Up

On March 4, 1993, former N.C. State basketball coach Jimmy Valvano gave a speech at the ESPYs (Excellence in Sports Performance Yearly) that people recite every day somewhere in the world. As he took the stage that night, he was living out his last days. His body was riddled with cancerous tumors and many didn't think he'd have the strength to accept the Arthur Ashe Courage and Humanitarian Award in New York City.

He accepted the award and gave one of the most memorable speeches I've seen in my lifetime. For more than 10 minutes he spoke about his life, dealing with cancer and his hope that one day a cure would be found and lives would be saved, even though he knew it would likely come after his death.

As he closed out his speech, Valvano said, "To be enthusiastic every day and as Ralph Waldo Emerson said, 'Nothing great could be accomplished without enthusiasm,' to keep your dreams alive in spite of problems whatever you have. The ability to be able to work hard for your dreams to come true, to become a reality."

A few weeks later, Jimmy V died at the age of 47. Though his life was relatively short, I would argue that few people lived with more passion, courage, and strength than Coach Valvano. He never gave up in his fight against cancer, and he set a great example for all of us to follow. Even in his final days, he wasn't quitting. He was doing everything he could to help find a cure for cancer, even though it would not save his own life. I get emotional just thinking about it.

The V Foundation for Cancer Research was born that night. More than $150 million has been raised by the V Foundation for cancer research. The number keeps climbing because of Coach Valvano and the lives he touched.

"Don't give up, don't ever give up," Jimmy V said. What if we all said that when we woke up each day? What if that was the mantra we used to start our day?

I can't say it enough, if you don't quit you will get what you want. It might take years or decades, but if you don't quit you will get what you want. As long as there is hope, you can keep pushing for your dream.

The next time you get frustrated, discouraged or mad, I want you to take a step back and think about what it is you want. If you truly want it, then you will not give up. Remind yourself that if you give up, there is no chance that you will get what you desire. Keep pushing. Remember everybody we see daily is either going in or coming out of something bad in their lives. We are all dealing with stuff.

It is those who learn how to work through struggles that come out on top.

You can get exactly what you want. The trick is that you cannot quit. The choice is yours. I hope that you choose to work until you realize your dreams. Greatness is inside of you. Now, we have to find a way to bring it out of you and share it with the world!

Own your words and actions

Do you know a person that constantly talks about what they are "going" to do, but never seems to follow through with action? We are all guilty of this at times. I would like for you to start being very intentional with what you say out loud, to other people and to yourself. Make sure your words and your actions match up. If they don't, now is the perfect time to change that!

Words are a matter of life and death. They are that powerful. What you say can change the lives of others and make a defining impact on people. If you follow through on what you say, then you will be a leader and an influential person.

Conversely, if your actions don't match the promises you make then you are going to have problems. People will stop listening to your rhetoric. People will not follow your lead. They will essentially start ignoring you. You will sound like Charlie Brown's school teacher.

"Blah, Blah, Blah, Blah! Blah ... Blah!" Kill that noise and do something big!

If you are struggling with this, find a buddy to serve as your Chief Reminder Officer. Your CRO can serve as your own personal Jiminy Cricket. You can remind yourself by writing down tasks you need to complete. I beg you to do whatever it takes so that your words and actions are in clear alignment.

Your words will determine your thinking. They will have an impact on your emotions, decision making, habits and character. If you are able to deliver on what you say, then life will be so much easier for you. If you are going to take the time to talk about doing it, let's make sure we go ahead and deliver consistently!

WIN! Winning attitude

It's 6 a.m. on Monday, and the alarm clock starts screaming at you. You reach over and slap it into submission as you wipe the sleep out of your eyes. You look out the window and it is raining cats and dogs. The dog is barking and wants to be let outside. You remember that you drank the last bit of coffee you had left on Sunday morning. Your next thought is all the things you HAVE to do during the upcoming day.

How is your attitude after hearing this scenario?

Here's how I would respond to all the potential negative thought above.

"Waaaaaahhhhhhooooooo!"

I'm alive for another day. I'd put my feet on the floor,

stand up and let the world know that I was a lucky man. I was born in America, and I've got 18 more hours on this day to do amazing things and help people. Oh, and I will get paid to do it. Now that is a program I like!

When you wake up each day, start telling yourself you are going to win. Long before you can win, you have to develop a winning attitude.

Drop the self-defeat and self-doubt mumbo jumbo. Nobody wants to hear that mess. Pick up a dose of self-empowerment and put on your "I WILL" attitude.

The most powerful voice in your world is the one inside your head. Train yourself to have a winning mentality and see if life doesn't start getting better for you. If you make the commitment to have a winning attitude then your chances of success are dramatically higher than if you mope and pout about when you face an obstacle. In fact, stop calling it an obstacle and consider it an opportunity. One of the characteristics of a successful person lies in their attitude.

Muhammad Ali. Michael Jordan. Roger Federer.

They are three of the greatest athletes ever in their respective sports. When they were in their prime, you better believe they had winning attitudes. There were certainly days where they probably didn't want to get out of bed, train and perform, but we never saw it because of the attitude they brought to work. Don't be afraid of failure. Act out of faith not fear. Exercise a winning attitude until it is part of who you are. See if people don't take notice. When you walk into a room, let people know you are a winner. Laugh a lot. Smile until your face hurts. Talk to everybody you see and ask them how they are doing. Bounce up and down if you need to get your mind right. Do whatever it takes to be positive and carry a winning attitude.

For the most part, people love or hate the New York Yankees. Entering the 2017 season, the Bronx Bombers had won 18 division titles, 40 American League pennants, and 27 World Series championships – all Major League Baseball records.

If you took a poll among avid baseball fans and asked why people love or hate the Yankees, the answer would be the same simple response.

It seems like all the Yankees do is win!

I want you to be like the New York Yankees in your world. Be a winner. Win so much that people admire, respect, and love you. Win so much that people don't like it because they are living their own life out of fear and not going after it like it was life or death.

Winning never gets old! Anybody that tells you that hasn't won very much. Life is not like little league sports where everybody gets a trophy now just for showing up. You are only as good as your latest victory. The past is just that ... the past! Focus on what you are doing now, not what you've done in the past. None of that matters if you want to really be successful.

You can't buy success. You can rent it, but remember that the rent is due daily. Think about that for a minute. Are you renting success on a daily basis? If you are, then you are doing the things that less successful people aren't willing to do. Embrace that logic and use your winning attitude to pay rent every single day.

RIGHT NOW

When people ask me if my path to success has been worth it, I don't even hesitate to tell them, "YES!!!" I thank God every single day that I decided I was not going to quit. That is still my mentality.

I've achieved some goals, but I continue setting new goals along the way. If you want to be successful, you are going to face some interesting situations. How you respond to the hurdles of life and business will determine if you stay on the path to success.

If you can focus on the principles and ideas presented in this chapter, I think you will start seeing positive results. I've seen and experienced a lot in the last 25 years, and I'm who I am today because I kept focusing on what was in front of me. Yes, I had long-term goals and a vision of what I wanted my life to be like. It's important to have big dreams, but you have to take action RIGHT NOW to reach your ultimate goals and dreams.

I encourage you to see the positives and not the negatives

when you weigh out a risk versus reward proposition. Focus on finding a way to ignite the spark inside you to win. Don't be afraid of working hard for what you truly want in life. Operate with a great heart that is needed for anybody with a bigger dream.

Don't be afraid to take chances on people who tell you how bad they want to be successful. Please don't ever give up! Own your words and your actions daily and carry yourself with a winning attitude in everything that you do.

You have the same 24 hours a day as the rest of the world. What you do with it is up to you. Don't be afraid to shoot for your goals and dreams. Everything that you want in life can be yours if you are willing to continue working toward your ultimate goal.

May your tomorrow always be better than your today. Shickyboom!

CHAPTER

10

"The entrepreneur always searches for change, responds to it, and exploits it as an opportunity."
- Peter Drucker

Future Of Business In America

One thing that I have always known is that you have to adopt and change to stay ahead of the competitive curve in the business world. Laws change, people change and the world changes as technology and innovation move at lightning speed. You have to change or you will fall behind.

My company, The Alliance, has always worked hard to stay on the cutting edge, and we have a team of people that know we have to continue improving ourselves and our system. We've come a long way from working out of my basement in 2002. The change and growth has led us to growing from that cramped little basement to an ever-expanding campus with more than 150 employees in three different buildings in Burlington, N.C.

WHAT DO WE DO EXACTLY?

Do we sell insurance? Yes. Are some of those products an investment? Yes. We offer "bofum" or both of them. We aren't your granddaddy's insurance company, and financial products have changed and become more versatile when it comes to thinking about retirement and taking care of your family and loved ones.

We have great flexibility because we partner with more than 15 different insurance carriers, which allows us to offer a wide range of products to fit every possible need for our clients. We believe that is one area that sets apart from many other companies because we can pull from more than 15 different carriers to find exactly what works best for the client.

THE OPPORTUNITY FOR FINANCIAL FREEDOM

Beyond helping families across the United States, we offer people a chance to build a team and get paid very well for doing so. We have levels, and some people are turned off by that concept. However, we are not selling soap, vitamins or some $500 kit to get you started. We sell insurance and it is one of the most highly regulated industries, so we have to make sure we are in compliance in all 50 states when it comes to what we do on a daily basis. If we weren't reputable, there is no way that multi-billion-dollar companies would let us offer their products.

We have agents ranging from just getting started to those who have built big businesses and have reached agency manager status or higher with our company. It is no different than a factory that has production workers, supervisors, managers, department heads, vice presidents, and a CEO. The key with us is that we reward and promote based on what you "DO" and not who you know or how long you've been working with us. You are paid based on what you do, and the bigger you build it, the higher your income will grow. Agents can earn promotions every two months with us, and there is an enormous amount of opportunity to move up fast with The Alliance. It's a level playing field. If you hit the promotion guidelines, you get promoted. It's that simple.

Many people think their income is tied directly to only their personal efforts and production. That is not the case with our company. If you work to recruit a team and build a big organization, then you will be rewarded with promotions. Now, if you only want to sell that is fine. However, we encourage people to do the one thing we teach: Sell, Recruit and Build. It's really three things, but we like to say it is the ONE THING we do.

In this age of information overload, it has never been easier to find people … FAST! You've got social media, cell phones, etc. You have a network of people at your fingertips. If you want to build a massive team, it's there for the person who isn't afraid to work to build it.

Many people would consider this network marketing. That phrase tends to get a negative response from people who have had a bad experience with juices, vitamins, cosmetics, coupon books, etc.

Our business is far different than those where you are forced to stock up on products that wind up lining the wall of your garage or storage space in your home. We sell insurance not some product you have to buy cases of and force upon your friends and family to break even.

I'm not knocking people who sell vitamins or juice. I am saying that we are different because we sell insurance products that people in America need. The market in middle America is there and it is an underserved demographic that we are fighting to help.

Is there a real market need for what we do? Do people find value in what you offer?

Again, there is a tremendous void that needs to be addressed when it comes to providing insurance to middle-income families in the United States. Our clients contact us to let us know they need insurance coverage and we help them get the protection they want so badly.

Can you make a living doing this?

We've had people start with us and make more than $100,000 in less than a year. We have veteran agents that make more than $1 million annually. We have people that only do this part-time and they soon replace their annual income. It really depends on the individual and their specific goals.

Is this something YOU can do?

We believe that anybody can be successful with us. Now, we have a system and a strategy that works. If you are willing to work, use the system, and follow the blueprint; we think you can do this.

People need insurance. There are more than 320 million people in America and a great deal of them don't have any insurance. We provide a great service to people who lack insurance, and we protect families by filling out simple paperwork. We get them protected, and that gives them Peace of Mind. Nobody likes to think about death, but it is inevitable. Having insurance reinforces how you feel about your loved ones and it erases any doubt about what will happen to a family when they lose a family member, who is often the main source of income.

Our job is to help families prepare for the future. We offer great products that help people for the rest of their lives and to future generations. In return for doing this, our agents get compensated very well. This allows our agents to make a great living and set their own work schedule based on their goals and dreams.

Is it easy? Nothing is ever as easy as it seems. Our work involves getting a license, taking advantage of training we offer, continuing to learn as you go, and building your business every week.

MAD OR GLAD … WHAT WILL MAKE YOU DO IT?

I like to say YOU can build your business MAD or GLAD. The key is to find out which one motivates you more and do it that way. Either way, pick one and start working for results. A lot of people are looking for instant success.

It doesn't happen overnight. Yes, you can start out on a hot streak and make sales, but the key is to be steady and consistent in your efforts.

Are you willing to master the mundane? Are you willing to do the things that most people aren't willing to do? Can you consistently work and improve using our system? If you can do the basics, then you have an excellent shot to be extremely successful with us.

People will say negative things. There will be people who don't have success with us, give up, and quit. Those who are successful with us are those who keep working and don't get frustrated to the point where they give up.

People make the mistake of giving up on what they are doing when they are so close to having a breakthrough. If you were three feet from gold and gave up, how would you feel if the next person came along and finished what you started while you walked home with your hat in your hand with your head down? You have to be persistent in your work and never reach a point where you give up. You will never get what you want if you quit.

Remember, if it were easy then more people would be successful. I want you to be one of the people that keeps working hard and keeps pushing for your goals and dreams.

I have seen people succeed and I have seen people fail. It makes me happy and sad to know that this is reality. I'm sad for those who gave up when I knew they were so close to exploding.

I'm extremely happy for those who I watch struggle, but never give up and eventually reach their goals. It is the latter that seem to be most successful and build massive businesses with us.

Our opportunity is for people with a true entrepreneurial spirit that want to be their own boss and control how their days are spent. We get paid to sell and we get paid to build. Most business models don't afford you that opportunity.

There are trillions of dollars in our industry and the income potential is as high as you want it to be. You can earn five-figures, six-figures or seven-figures with us? It's really up to you to decide how much you want to make.

This business offers you the chance to be the boss, set your schedule, own a business, and discover financial freedom.

You can build it big or small. You can build it fast or slow. You can help a few people or invite the masses to join you. You can realize your dreams. You can give hope to others.

NOW is the time to decide what YOU want to do!

Are you ready to build it MAD or GLAD?

The time to decide is RIGHT NOW! How bad do you want it? Are you going to build it big?

Let's DO IT!

Get started NOW … RIGHT NOW!

Inside The Circle

CHAPTER

11

"Eighty percent of success is showing up."
- Woody Allen

Go To Grow

A few years ago I realized that we needed to create a location for people all around the country to be able to spend time together every single week. I took a U.S. map and pinpointed 70-plus cities and started planning how we could hold meetings on Mondays, Tuesdays, Wednesdays and Thursdays every week.

The result is what is now known as HotSpot meetings. I could not host 70 meetings in a week by myself and neither can any other person. However, the team, collectively, can and does do it together! The result was amazing and the team started realizing that we all could benefit from helping each other host this weekly meetings.

Instead of not knowing what was going on in each city, at each meeting, we now have a formula that is used at every meeting. If you live in Florida, you

can send people from all over the country to a meeting near where they live and they will get help from the team. At the same time, you could be helping a fellow agent with a new recruit in your area even if you don't even know the agent! We work together to make this happen and it's become a cornerstone for our people to spend time together every week.

These meetings are huge because of the training, association, and recognition they provided for the team. We've created a blueprint for these meetings and the meetings have proved to be highly successful for us helping get new people trained and started.

Before HotSpot meetings, people would ask me how I could get so many people to meetings I was hosting? In my mind, I never looked at it that way. I would often respond by saying, "I don't have that many. What you see are the people still left."

I have recruited thousands of people in this business and people come and go over time. It is part of the process and I don't let it bother me. People think I have a huge organization, and for most I guess I do. I don't think about it that way. I see my business as small compared to what I envision it being in the future.

HotSpots are one way that we make sure people are engaged and focused on being successful in our business. I can promise you that these meetings help eliminate some of the frustrations for new people because you can ask questions, get around people that are more successful, and learn things you don't know yet.

Why do people get frustrated and quit? They don't have a place that feels like home and they don't feel like they have an outlet to get the help they need. Our HotSpot meetings serve as a place where "everybody knows your name" and "they're always glad you came." Just like Cliff Claven and Norm Peterson on the show *Cheers*, our HotSpots are a place for people to come and not be judged for better or worse. It's a place where you can be yourself and be part of a team or family.

Why do I do this?

It makes a positive impact. It shows people that nobody is perfect because you get to hear the stories of people in the field trying to help families. It provides an environment where we can celebrate and recognize successes and failures – both big and small.

Woody Allen famously once said, "Eighty percent of success is showing up."

If you aren't attending HotSpot meetings and our national events, then you are not following one of The 8 Steps to Success: Attend All Meetings.

I can show you the top 250 agents in our business and I will guarantee you that each and every one of them attends weekly meetings and attends all big events. Some people cringe at the thought of having to go to a meeting every week. We have to change that mindset and attitude.

Here are some possible objections for not wanting to attend the meeting:

It takes too much time!

Yes, it takes time. It also takes time to learn how to do something. If you knew that attending the meeting would lead to you having a more profitable business, would that change your mind? Act like your business depends on you being at the meeting, because it really does. The meeting needs you, and you need the meeting. It works both ways.

Imagine that you have a typical 9-to-5 job. Your boss requires you to attend a weekly staff meeting and you are paid to be there. In this business, you are the boss. Tell yourself this meeting is important and put it in your calendar every week so that you know your "BOSS" expects you to be there.

Too many people have the employee mentality because it's what they have known for years. Make the decision to act like an entrepreneur and not an employee.

I'll try to make it …

No! When you say "try" you are leaving yourself an excuse to not make it to the meeting. This means you won't come every week because something will ultimately "come up" at the last minute. You can't just attend when it is convenient for you. You can't show up when you are free with no plans. You have to make the commitment because others are counting on you to be there. It only works when the entire team makes the effort every single week.

If you miss a meeting, that's OK. People are not going to beat you up over it. Things happen. The important thing is to consistently make sure you are at the meetings. You have a story to tell and people can help you get better at these meetings.

If you are truly serious about building a business, one of the things you need to be willing to do is attend a HotSpot meeting each week.

"Winning means you're willing to go longer, work harder and give more than anyone else."
Green Bay Packers coach Vince Lombardi

A Winning Attitude Becomes A Winning Habit

How many times have you heard a person tell you how badly they want something? The problem with most people is they say they want it bad, but they don't work to create winning habits.

If you have bad habits that limit your potential, you can't get better unless you work to change something. You have to be willing to go through tough times before you reach the finish line. You have to stop seeing challenges as obstacles and talk about them as opportunities instead.

It starts with your attitude. If you can adopt a positive attitude and start speaking positively, then you are more likely to pick up habits that will help you win. This involves changing, and most people don't want to change. Most people change when they are desperate or when they are inspired. Change doesn't happen overnight. You don't win instantly, and you don't lose immediately either.

If you eat fast food constantly you are going to see your health decline over time.

If you exercise daily and eat healthy, you are probably going to be in better shape than if you didn't do those things.

Whatever your behavior, things don't happen overnight. It's like Ernest Hemingway wrote of bankruptcy in his book "The Sun Also Rises," simply, "How did you go bankrupt? Two ways. Gradually, then suddenly."

If you start doing winning behaviors today, you will be closer to your goal tomorrow. If you keep doing it daily, it will eventually happen for you.

Gradually ... then suddenly!

The fastest way to change is to take action. This could be changing your circle of influence, changing your spending habits, working out more, etc.

GET YOUR MIND RIGHT

When you know a meeting is coming, you need to start

getting your mind right before you get to the meeting.

Maybe your conscience starts asking you, "Is the meeting really that important? Can I skip it and be OK? You could be doing so many other things, you know that?"

When this happens, remember what your goal is and what you are working for. Remember somebody at that meeting needs you there. Be a leader that comes to the meeting and adds value for others.

Don't let your mind talk you out of doing what you know you should do. If you allow your mind to talk you out of going to a meeting, what will happen when you have a rough day in the field with clients? Don't let your mind talk you out of business!

One of the things I don't look forward to when I wake up in the morning is getting on the elliptical and working out. I have to talk myself into working out daily. One way I do this is by putting it on my calendar. My calendar controls what I do so I make sure it is on my calendar.

Make every effort to get your mind focused on the positives of being at the meeting. Put it on your calendar and be there.

WHY HAVE MEETINGS?

Our success is based on a system that we've spent years creating. Part of that formula is weekly meetings and national events. These are the places where people make big decisions to change their lives for the better. It's where they get inspired or angry about where they are and it is where they make sweeping changes.

We are all building businesses. We are also building people and relationships. HotSpot meetings are a place for training, associating, motivating, and recognizing people.

How many times have you heard a player or coach during an interview after a big win talk about why they were ready when the moment presented itself in the big game?

Time and time again, the star player or genius coach has roughly the same answer: "We won because we were prepared when the opportunity came."

The best have practiced it, executed it, and talked about seemingly forever before they ever have the chance to actually do it in a game. That's what separates winning and losing.

There is a fine line between being a hero and a zero in life. If you train and do the little things repeatedly, you will be ready when it is your time to shine.

You are on the team and the team needs people to set the example. New recruits will mirror what you do. If you come to meetings, they will come to meetings. You have the chance to set the example … will you set a good or bad example? New recruits don't know how everything works and it is important that you show them the way.

You know that you are not perfect, but a new agent doesn't necessarily know that. Be the leader that keeps people on the right track. In doing so, you will also hold yourself accountable.

ARE YOU IN?

We talked earlier about the word "try." It is a very dangerous word because it sits squarely on the fence, not committed to either side. At some point, you have to pick what room you are in: the room for the committed or the room for the uncommitted. Our business has people in both rooms, but there is far more room for you in the room for the COMMITTED.

I grew up loving North Carolina State University and Wolfpack athletics. When people ask me who I cheer for, I don't hesitate. I am COMMITTED to the Wolfpack. No doubt about it!

I have been married to my wife, Jane for almost 30 years. I don't "try" to be a husband. I'm COMMITTED.

We have a daughter, Haleigh and a son, Spencer. I don't "try" to be their father. I'm their daddy. I'm COMMITTED.

None of those things are negotiable for me. They are part of who I am, my life, and my purpose.

The Albrights meeting a lion in Africa

Stop "TRYing" to do things. Let's go ahead and COMMIT. Life will be easier when you do that. Don't even give it a second thought. Don't have a conversation in your head about why or why not. JUST DO IT. You do it and keep doing it until it is like taking a shower in the morning. It becomes a habit. Your team will see that you are committed and they will follow your lead.

The habit will take hold and you will start seeing victories come because of the training and work you are doing.

I don't miss meetings and events that are on my calendar. I made that decision years ago and it has paid off over the years in ways I can't even explain to you. I encourage you to find ways to show you are committed and keep working at it.

Meetings are part of the business. They are part of our system. The team controls the meetings and they are a key part of our level of success.

When you GO, you will GROW. As you grow, you will learn how to help others grow too. When the team keeps growing, that's when the level of success we all enjoy goes through the roof and high into the sky. Make sure you are part of that explosion. The rewards will be worth all the effort you put into it.

CHAPTER

"The best and most beutiful things in the world cannot be seen or even touched--they must be felt with the heart."'
- Helen Keller

Four Ways To Grab A Heart

Have you ever felt a sudden urge to help a person who you know is hurting? You can feel that they have a heavy heart, their mind is racing in a negative way, and they need somebody to help them fix what is broken.

When you can grab a person's heart and mind, then you can change their life. Life as they know it will never be the same … and in a good way.

MOTIVATION

Mo-ti-va-tion: the act or process of giving someone a reason for doing something – the act or process of motivating someone – the condition of being eager to act or work – the condition of being motivated – a force or influence that causes someone to do something

"Merriam-Webster" dictionary definition of Motivation

What motivates a person? The first step is to find out what moves a person. When you know what drives them, you can quickly speak to them about subjects that will spawn action. People who are able to get people to move or take action are the highest paid people in the world. If you can inspire a person to do something, watch out! Leaders get people to move … quickly.

If you can pinpoint what drives a person or gets them motivated, then you can help them get what they want. Now, a person is easier to do this with if they have a great attitude and are not afraid to exert the effort it takes for a specific task.

You have to get people to realize they are not authorized or allowed to quit, get frustrated or perturbed. You can, however, make it clear that they are more than welcome to ACT, make adjustments along the way and then act again. Let them know everything will be OK, and obstacles are really just opportunities dressed unpleasantly. Keep smiling and assure them that together you can work through any problem until you fix it.

Make the challenge fun and easy.

It's been said over and over that people don't care how much you know until they know how much you care. This is the first step in capturing a person's heart and mind.

Show people through verbal and even physical displays of affection, like a handshake or a hug, that you care. Be a person who is willing to show others that you appreciate them and are going to help them along their journey.

Maybe you call them randomly to give them a quick pep talk. This will blow a person's mind if it has never happened to them. It shows you truly care and that you are going to work with them when you should and, at times, when it is not expected.

Keep smiling. The world likes you more when you smile.

Let people know how much you enjoy life and the people in your life. Tell people how much you enjoy being around them. If you are building a team, treat people like teammates and not robots doing a job or trying to make sales. Treat people as people, first and foremost. It makes a huge difference to you, the person, and the team.

CONFIDENCE

Con-fi-dence: a feeling or belief that you can do something well or succeed at something – a feeling or belief that someone or something is good or has the ability to succeed at something – the feeling of being certain that something will happen or that something is true.

When a person is confident, they believe they can move mountains. Part of being confident is knowing that you have the necessary skills to produce the outcome you desire. Confidence is simply a movement pattern. It's just motions when you break it all down. The belief factor takes us more to the mental part of confidence. People have to believe they can do something or they can't. You have to believe you can do it.

When we lack confidence, it doesn't mean we don't have the ability needed to perform. It really means we lack or lost the faith to do something. You can help people struggling with this by encouraging them. Writing a quick note or email helps. Take a moment to speak to them face-to-face. Tell them you are proud of them and that you know they can do whatever it is they are working for. Help them raise their own belief level by being a cheerleader for them.

Humans are often guilty of listening to negative voices. I call them faith and belief stealers. We've all had people like this in our life. They spend all their energy and effort talking about all the things that can't be done. If these people would focus on positive outcomes and completing small tasks, far more would be achieved.

Real achievers operate from the heart first. When you start with the heart, then the head follows. Human thinking, reasoning and logic can disrupt a person's heart. Your head will fight your heart, and negative words and thoughts make it even worse.

Avoid negative people and negative talk. Treat it like a stop light. When the negative is around you, hit the brakes and act like you are at a red light. Red lights are a waste of your time. Work hard to stop as soon as you encounter them.

When you hear positive talk or get around positive people, hit the gas and keep trucking! Positivity is a green light on the highway to success. You can't have enough green lights when you are working to be successful.

I have great news for you. When you hear people saying things like, "it's tradition … history tells us … or that's just the way it is," you don't have to buy into their logic!!! We are all a mess, just look around, but God performs miracles through people like you and me. If it were easy, it wouldn't be a miracle, right?

How else does a brown cow eat green grass, produce white milk that turns into yellow butter? I have no idea, but I like milk with brownies and butter on biscuits. Belief is acting not understanding. You are never going to know everything so why waste time on silly details?

Accept that you are not perfect, nor do you need to be perfect. Keep making mistakes and keep trying things. If you try something and it doesn't work, then just hang on. Tie a knot in the end of the rope and don't let go.

The only way to reach your desired destination is to keep going.

You will get there eventually.

EMOTION

Emo-tion: the affective aspect of consciousness – a state of feeling.

Emotions far too often get the best of us. Even when we feel it happening, it is very difficult to control our emotions. Controlling our emotions can make all the difference in the world when it comes to our success. Our emotions affect our ability to perform and alter our behavior in every area of our life. Emotion is a response to something that's going on deeper inside a person. When you are working with people, stuff will happen. Don't compound things by becoming frustrated. Don't react with the wrong type of emotion.

Psychologically, people who are emotional might laugh, cry or scream. They might lose focus. They might lack motivation. Behaviorally, emotional people will pout, rant, give up, etc.

Successful people know that how YOU behave is exactly who you are.

Seek out pleasant people and avoid unpleasant people. Unpleasant people are negative. They operate in a world filled with frustration, blame, anger, fear, and disappointment. Pleasant people are happy, excited, joyful, and love life.

Remember how powerful emotions can be because they can HELP or hurt. You can control the direction you let them take you. Steer toward the positive and pleasant side of the road. Stop the emotions that hurt and work hard to increase the emotions that help downplay bad things and eliminate the negative. Cultivate good emotions and life will be much better for you and the people in your life.

COHESION

Co-he-sion: the act or state of sticking together tightly

To build a winning team, there has to be great chemistry, camaraderie, and cohesion. It has to be a group of people working toward a common goal. The physical and emotional unification of a team in pursuit of a singular goal is a great way to define team cohesion.

This means finding people that don't think they are entitled to anything. It is assembling a group of people that don't expect something, and don't feel like they are owed something. You can't build a team with individuals that think if they perform they better get something in return. That won't work.

Team cohesion happens when the group moves from having an "all about ME" mindset to a "WE not me" attitude. This cohesion is created over time and it starts with your attitude, your heart, and your willingness to leave your ego in the past.

PULLING IT TOGETHER

When you can help a person find their motivation, build up their confidence, control their emotions, and buy into team cohesion, there is nothing you can't achieve. You will not only enjoy an amazing life, but help others do the same.

When you grab the hearts and minds of people, you will experience success in an environment that places long-term relationships as a higher priority than short-term achievement. When it is all said and done, your life is measured by the company you kept more so than any amount of money you earned.

I encourage you to focus on grabbing people's hearts and making them understand that they are important to you. Love people the way you love yourself. That's about as much as I could ask of you. If you don't do anything else, please make it your goal to love people in a genuine manner. When you do this consistently, you will be rewarded in ways you never imagined. It will blow your mind and you will leave a lasting impact on people.

That's my ultimate dream!

My goal is to leave a legacy that others will follow and carry on what we started back in 2002. We know that love conquers all and that legacy is the goal that will carry each of us into eternity when we take our final breath on earth.

I want to leave this world with people shaking their heads in amazement when they think about what we accomplished during our brief time here.

My dream is for as many people as possible to live life that way and I want to help them go as far as they possibly can. We are going to help people. We are going to make a difference. We are going to have a heckuva time doing it too!

I want to leave this world knowing that people knew who we were, and that The Alliance was the vehicle we used to change the world for the better.

CHAPTER

13

*"I hated every minute of training, but I said,
'Don't quit. Suffer now and live the rest of
your life as a champion.'"*
- Muhammad Ali

Ultimate Duty Is …

One of my heroes Jim Rohn said, "Whatever good things we build end up building us."

You can easily have a building constructed that is massive and impressive to those who view it with the human eye. But, for me, there is nothing as satisfying as seeing a person reach their full potential in business.

A building can be taken down faster than it is erected. To create a solid, stable foundation, it will take great effort and energy. When it is done correctly, the results are impressive. It is done brick by boring brick. One a time. Over and over.

By putting each brick in place and laying a foundation, something is created. It can be mundane and boring, but you have to see the bigger picture that comes through dogged,  repeated effort to make it something big. There will be imperfections, but that's OK. You might break a brick and have to replace it with a new one. That's OK. You have to keep plugging away even when you experience setbacks. As long as you never give up, you are going to end up with great results.

A person built with a solid work ethic, strong principles, big dreams and an abundant vision is one of the most powerful and impressive images you'll witness in this life. A person who continues to grow, never gives up, and keeps pushing is hard to keep down. Learning should never stop. There is not one person in the world who ever knew everything. The quest for knowledge never ends for the person that is truly growing and trying to be the best person they can in life.

I never get tired of seeing the next success story with The Alliance because I've been there myself. I know how gratifying the journey is going from being broke to being rich in terms of finances and relationships. I thank God for the journey thus far. When I see a person with big dreams, it makes me dream bigger and inspires me to do more. When you get around a team of people that think that way then things get crazy good.

People ask me why I keep working so hard, why I am not content with the many blessings in my life and why I don't slow down? The answer is simple: I'm not done helping other people get what they want in life. It's too much fun. I'd rather wear out than rust in the rain sitting on the porch doing nothing. There's too much greatness in the world for me to waste my talents.

So, that's my mission: help more people. I'm expanding my mission from coast to coast for anybody that has a dream and isn't afraid to work hard. When I started, I knew that I could make it work for me, and I also learned that I can help others do the same thing. If you are reading this, I invite YOU to join me on the road to success. It starts inside the circle with YOU!

Part of helping a person is figuring out where they are NOW and where they want to go in the future. That's not an easy question to answer for a lot of people. It involves looking at yourself and all your imperfections and deciding what you are willing to change if it means getting what you truly want in life.

Once I find out where people are and what they want, the fun part begins. YOU have to WORK to get better, to get what you want, to chase the ultimate prize.

Can you really build a person? That's a complex question, but I believe you can. Will you invest time and efforts in people and be disappointed with the end results? Yes. It has happened to me a thousand times. You have to have short-term amnesia when it happens and keep looking for the next person to help.

When you are trying to build a team and build people, you have to remember that it is a numbers game when you are recruiting. I'm always hopeful that somebody is going to make it big. I believe we all want to believe in people.

Over time, you realize that some people don't want it as much as you think they do. I have to focus my efforts on those who are "Doing the Do" that shows me they want it. I have to let others marinate in the room of the uncommitted and that is painful at times. It's part of the growing pains involved in building a big organization. I can't stop working on my dream while I wait on other people to figure it out. I'm not mad at those people and I'm patient and nice about it. However, I've got a lot more I plan to get done before my time is through.

Most people that you recruit won't last. Accept that and don't worry about it. Others will stay and you will have relationships and friendships with them that make all the disappointment worth the effort. You have to stay steady and consistent in what you are doing regardless of what happens outside of your circle. Focus on the things you can control and impact — YOU! — and let the things you cannot control go by the wayside. Life will be easier when you do that.

Building a business and people is never easy. If it were, everybody would do it. If you want to have a healthy garden, you've got to toss a lot of seed on the ground to get the crop you seek down the road. You need rain to help you out and you are going to have to add water on your own to help cultivate the right environment for your garden to grow. The more you plant and nurture, the more you will see your garden grow. Every summer my family grows a garden. It takes more than just my hands to make it happen. Even after the seeds are planted, the work is just starting. We set up an irrigation system to help us maintain things like tomatoes, squash, potatoes, broccoli and peppers – just to name a few of the items we grow.

We water and we watch. We wait. Eventually, we start seeing results. Even then, the garden goodies have to be picked before they go bad. There are animals like deer and squirrels that "steal" food even though they know we don't like them doing this. We can't completely stop that, but we consistently make trips to the garden in an effort to limit the amount they take from our hard work.

Being able to enjoy the results of working our garden leads to us having fresh produce that many people must drive to a grocery store to pick up. We just walk a 100 feet or so and pick what we want right out of the garden. I love it and look forward to having that garden every year. It's a process to do it, but it is well worth it when the fruits and veggies are on the vine!

It is the same with The Alliance. It takes time, effort, emotion, energy, and the right attitude. People are funny creatures.

You can't assume that something is being done because you ask them to do something one time. Communication and overcommunication are required to help a person get in the habit of doing the right tasks and activities.

Ignore those who question you and say you cannot do something. Those people don't matter because they can't see the picture you are painting. Don't fear change. Embrace it and keeping growing. The better you become, the better your teammates will become. They will follow your lead, so be the best leader you can be.

Take advantage of all the tools, resources and the system we've put in place. These are items that I've used to become successful and we've put them in place to help you succeed.

I believe you can build people. We see it in sports, the military and in business. You can push a person beyond where they think they can go and you can help them accomplish more than they believe is possible in their mind.

Don't be afraid to be a great teammate. At times, this means you have to have difficult or tough conversations about behaviors and ions. You are not perfect and neither is anybody else, but if you are helping a person then there is nothing wrong with pulling a teammate to the side and constructively having a conversation.

It takes great effort to build a person. When you do this successfully, you will be glad you did. The payoff will be worth every ounce of blood, sweat, and tears you put in. When you figure out how to do this effectively, life becomes more fun and you start to understand what it means to win ... and win big!

FIND PEOPLE WHO WANT TO BUILD

If YOU want to be a builder, we can show you how it is done. There are people who don't want to build, and we can't make them want to do it. Those who are committed to building are who we are focused on, and that is where the majority of our time is spent. Your job is to find teammates that want it and work with them to make their dream a reality.

LONG ROAD AHEAD

Building doesn't happen overnight. It never has. It happens gradually then suddenly ... even if it seems like it took no time or forever. It can take years. It starts with one person and it grows from there. There will be mistakes, headaches, and disasters. Keep learning, working and pushing and never, ever quit.

I have great news about our system. It can be duplicated. You build a person and then they do the same with another person. The cycle continues as it evolves and grows over time.

If you are committed to building a business, your ultimate duty is to help others do the same. Help another person because somebody did the same for you earlier. The reward for this is having freedom and flexibility to live a rich and healthy life.

My ultimate duty is to keep doing the same. I will lead by example and show others that the mission is very possible. The dream is very real. The vision has been cast for all of us to realize our potential.

The journey I am on is not one I take lightly. It is a great responsibility. Make it your mission to work hard to find great people who want the best that life can offer. It is an honor to work in an industry where the focus of what we do is centered around helping people.

I am honored and blessed to be in an amazing business that has led me to where I am today. From a young age, I believed I was destined to do great things and I never shied away from work. I am far from finished. My dreams and goals keep getting bigger and bigger.

I'm proud of the system we have in place, but you haven't seen nothing yet. We will continue to Sell, Recruit and Build! I hope YOU are ready to help me on this journey as we continue growing the dreams of The Alliance! **YOU** are Inside the Circle, and that's where it all begins! RIGHT NOW! Go Get You Some!!!

ACKNOWLEDGMENTS

This book is a result of the hard work of many people. When you set the goal of publishing a book, that's the easy part. There are so many little things that go into the final product, and I wanted to use this space to say thanks to my team for making Inside The Circle a reality.

There are two people in particular that made this book happen. My writer Mac Heffner spent countless hours taking my concepts and ideas and putting them on paper. He made additions, edits and kept tweaking the book during the process. He is around me a lot and is pretty good at taking a simple idea from me and creating more content based off an idea.

My wife Jane was also heavily involved in the final version of the book. She helped tremendously when it came to making sure the contents of the book were what we wanted to say, and she is a great editor.

I have to thank my daughter Haleigh for helping with the illustrations in the book. It's pretty neat to be able to partner with your daughter to help your book better. She did a great job and I'm happy she wanted to help us out.

I want to thank our creative team – specifically our creative director Jay Daugherty and designer Ryan Wagner – for their work on this project too. Through the editing and design process, they were able to deliver the final product you now hold in your hands.

Special thanks goes to Missy Stipetich and Amber Bowen, who both help keep me doing what I am supposed to be doing and when I'm supposed to be doing it. You couldn't ask for two better executive assistants.

To my staff, thanks for all you do. To be successful, it takes a team and teamwork. We have a great team and I'm proud of what we've built at our home office. Thanks to each of you for helping me chase my dreams! We're just getting started and there's more to come in the future!

To you, the reader, for taking the time to read my book. I hope you enjoyed it and I look forward to writing the next one soon.

Sincerely,

ABOUT THE AUTHOR

Andy Albright is the president and CEO of The Alliance, a motivational speaker and coach, and the author of "The 8 Steps to Success," and "Millionaire Maker Manual." Albright is involved with numerous charities and organizations.

Albright is a proud graduate of North Carolina State University, and is the namesake of the Albright Entrepreneurs Village (AEV), a place for NC State students who want to learn to think like an entrepreneur. The AEV is a residential community on Centennial Campus that involves residents from all majors and provides social and co-curricular activities to engage them in the startup world and encourage them to develop their ideas and ventures. This diverse group receives coaching from successful entrepreneurs and immersion in the programs that help students translate ideas into action.

In November of 2016, Andy and his wife, Jane pledged a $5 million gift to bolster both the NC State Entrepreneurship Initiative and the General H. Hugh Shelton Leadership Center. In honor of this extraordinary commitment, Innovation Hall — which opened on Centennial Campus in 2014 — is now known as Andy and Jane Albright Innovation Hall. One component of the Albrights' gift is an endowment for the Albright Entrepreneurs Village, a Living and Learning Village the Burlington, North Carolina, couple previously established. NC State's Living and Learning Villages are interest-based communities that engage students inside and outside the classroom.

Albright is a member of the advisory board for NC State's Entrepreneurship Initiative, a member of the advisory board for the NC State University Engagement and a loyal supporter and major donor of Wolfpack athletics. Albright is a motivational speaker for various groups and organizations. He is passionate about helping mentor entrepreneurial-minded students and aspiring job creators.

Albright's company is one of the country's largest and most successful insurance marketing organizations, specializing in life event marketing and sales. Andy has appeared in regional North Carolina magazines and newspapers, and his company was selected from a pool of 35,000 area businesses as the N.C. Triad's Fastest Growing Company by Greensboro's Triad Business Journal in 2007. Albright was named to the Triad's 2011 Movers & Shakers list by Business Leader magazine, and has appeared on several national radio shows.

Andy and his wife, Jane live in Union Ridge, N.C. They have two children – Haleigh (2017 NC State graduate) and Spencer (2017 graduate of The Tilton School in New Hampshire and member of the Class of 2021 at NC State).

ABOUT THE ILLUSTRATOR

Haleigh Albright is a 2017 graduate of North Carolina State University, where she earned a Bachelor of Arts degree in Communication with a concentration in public relations and a minor in Business Administration. She is currently pursuing a post-graduate degree in Global Luxury Management through NC State. As an undergraduate at NC State, Haleigh was the Vice President of Membership for NC State's Panhellenic Association and the Recruitment Director for the Alpha Kappa Chapter of Chi Omega.

Haleigh has an entrepreneurial spirit and work ethic. She used her talents to acquire work on top of her studies during her time in Raleigh, N.C. She worked in event planning for Raleigh-based companies La Fete and The Merrimon-Wynn House.

Additionally, Haleigh has used her artistic skills to provide calligraphy as a freelance artist, and supplied artwork for Wake Forest Baptist Medical Center's Holiday Cards for a number of years to send to donors and patients.

Haleigh is the proud daughter of Andy and Jane Albright and is the proud owner of Ava, her four-legged, Australian Shepherd sidekick.

She plans to take over the world!

Millionaire Maker Manual

A MUST READ BOOK FOR Alliance AGENTS.

Andy Albright, the "millionaire maker" CEO, wrote this book to serve as a "greenprint" for Alliance agents to MAXIMIZE results in sales and recruiting.

In the MMM, you'll discover:

- The importance of the 4 Basics of Recruiting
- The power of using your Activity book
- How to go from 1 to 11 in 1 Step
- How to get referrals by asking questions
- How to properly set up a meeting room
- The WAY to Show The Plan
- Available on audio
- AND SO MUCH MORE!!!

Andy's "Green Book" is the most complete tool for any Alliance agent looking to boost his/her business and income level.

Millionaire Maker Manual
-by Andy Albright
Retail $29.95

ALLIANCE PODCASTS

GET NEW EPISODES
AUTOMATICALLY TO YOUR DEVICES

GOOGLE PLAY   PODCAST   STITCHER

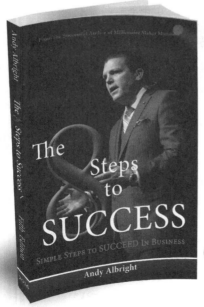

The 8 Steps To Success
by Andy Albright

Simple Steps To SUCCEED In Business

**Go to ShopAtNAA.com to
get yours today!**

ANDY ALBRIGHT CD SERIES

5 Ways To Stay Positive

In life, we all face challenges. Andy will give you 5 strategies to stay positive when you face obstacles.

How To Overcome It All

Life is filled with struggles and you have to overcome the obstacles of life or your will get stuck in the mess.

MOVE - Volume 1

This mix tape-style audio will help you start your day off right or get your mind right when you are riding in your car or working out.

MOVE - Volume 2

The follow up to MOVE 1, this mix tape features short inspirational tracks to inspire you no matter what you are doing.

Thrive

Go to ShopAtNAA.com to get yours today!

This 3-disc set of audios offers high-level training to help you grow and avoid

FREE!

SELF-EVALUATION TEST!

Do you have what it takes to make your dreams come true?

"Dreams come a size too big so that we can grow into them." –Josie Bisset

Do you have a dream? Thinking you want to go after it? What do you do next? Would you like to know if you have a chance to obtain it?

I have great news for you...Visit <u>AndyAlbright.com</u> to get a free overview and evaluation to see if you have what it takes!

Take my quick, simple and easy evaluation and find out today!